THE TRINITY AND CHRISTIAN DEVOTION

THE TRINITY AND CHRISTIAN DEVOTION

by

CHARLES W. LOWRY

M.A.(Harv.), D.Phil.(Oxon.)

Rector of All Saints' Church, Chevy Chase, Maryland
Sometime Professor of Systematic Divinity in the
Virginia Theological Seminary

LONDON
EYRE AND SPOTTISWOODE

TRINITARIAN BELIEF

CHARLES W. LOWRY: *The Trinity and Christian Devotion.* Eyre and Spottiswoode. 4s. 6d.

So much of our current devotional literature is sentimental and intellectually incoherent that any attempt to base Christian devotion upon clearly thought-out theological principles deserves the warmest welcome. Nobody who is capable of following a closely argued, if in places somewhat highly compressed and breathless, presentation of the fundamental doctrine of the Christian Faith will fail to profit by this book.

Dr. Lowry sees plainly that trinitarian belief is, historically as well as rationally, at the heart of the primitive Christian gospel. And it is a belief that demands, and indeed generates, its own intellectual formulation. Dr. Lowry offers a drastic criticism of the question-begging and misleading statement, so often repeated in recent years, that revelation is given not in propositions but in acts; the doctrine of the Trinity he tells us, " came into existence as an integral *accompaniment* of certain unexpected events that shook, first, the souls of a few elect men, and then the world itself, to the foundations," and he insists that " accompaniment " and not " implication " is the word to use. Again, he affirms that " there is no alternative to positing, in the full light of modern criticism, a special inspiration of Holy Scripture," though he makes little reference to the consequences that may be expected to follow a whole-hearted return to this traditional Biblical attitude, beyond a recognition of the intricacy of the problem raised by modern study.

The outstanding impression that this book leaves is of the fullness of content and width of application that are to be found in trinitarian belief. The richness, fecundity and intensity of Christian life are seen as derived from the nature of the God in whom Christians believe and whom they adore. It may well be suspected that the impoverishment and devitalization of much present-day Anglo-Saxon religion are a direct result of its lack of foundation in classical Christian dogma; to this Dr. Lowry offers a welcome antidote. If there are places where we should like to see his thought more fully developed —as in his references to Original Sin— this is no doubt due to the limits imposed upon him by the size of the book.

Times Literary Supplement
May 11. 1946

THIS BOOK (FIRST PUBLISHED IN 1946) IS PRODUCED IN COMPLETE CONFORMITY WITH THE AUTHORIZED ECONOMY STANDARDS AND IS MADE AND PRINTED IN GREAT BRITAIN FOR EYRE AND SPOTTISWOODE (PUBLISHERS) LIMITED, 15 BEDFORD STREET LONDON, W.C.2, BY BILLING AND SONS LTD., GUILDFORD AND ESHER

INTRODUCTION

THIS is the last of a series of Lent Books arranged by the late Dr. William Temple, in which, from the beginning, I had the privilege of being his co-editor. The series began six years ago, when he was at York, and he continued it when he became Primate of all England.

The subject of this book was suggested to Dr. Lowry by the Archbishop himself. In his introduction to the first volume in the series—the Master of Balliol's book on *The Two Moralities*—his Grace said that there is a danger that religious devotion and intellectual enterprise should fall apart; no study could more fitly find a place in a series designed to meet that danger than this one of the doctrine of the Trinity and Christian Devotion.

William Temple was one of the leaders of World Christianity. It was no accident, then, that two of the writers in this series were not members of the Anglican Church. And when he went to Canterbury he said that if the series was to be continued, its net must be cast very widely. It was a special satisfaction to him to find in the American Episcopal Church a writer, known personally to himself, whose published work was of outstanding intellectual distinction.

Dr. Lowry's book is a real contribution to the understanding of the Christian religion, and I shall be surprised if many do not find the reading of it an enrichment of their experience, as well as a discipline for their thinking. Dr. Lowry has taken the trouble to be lucid and, in my judgment, his book deserves to rank with the best in the series.

ALBERT E. BAKER

TO THE MEMORY OF

CHARLES WESLEY LOWRY

MY FATHER ACCORDING TO THE FLESH AS IN LOVE

AND

WILLIAM TEMPLE

PHILOSOPHER, ARCHBISHOP, FATHER-IN-GOD, AND FRIEND

PREFACE

THE late Archbishop of Canterbury, Dr. William Temple, did me great honour in inviting me two years ago to write his Lent Book for 1946. This honour has been augmented since, for the presiding Bishop of the Episcopal Church in the United States of America, the Right Reverend Henry St. George Tucker, has graciously adopted my book for his own Lent Book in 1946.

I can but record in simple words my sense of gratitude to these great Churchmen for the confidence placed in me. I am only too aware of its slender foundation in reality, and of my inadequacy in the face of the lofty issues raised by the doctrine which is at once the ultimate mystery and the supreme glory of the Christian Faith. Yet I am sure that no more fruitful theme, or one more calculated, in spite even of halting discourse and limping intellectual gait, to draw the attention of men and women in this troubled generation to the only source of inward renewal, clarity and beatitude, could have been chosen.

The subject of this volume was suggested by Dr. Temple when he invited me to write it for Lent, 1946. The reasons for his choice of theme and writer lay mainly in the fact that I wrote during the years 1930-31 and 1931-32 and submitted in partial satisfaction of the requirements of the degree of Doctor of Philosophy at Oxford University a dissertation on the doctrine of the Trinity. During the Edinburgh Conference in 1937 His Grace, the Archbishop, Chairman of the Conference, with characteristic generosity and thoughtful interest in the concerns of others, spent some of the very few spare moments he could have had in examining a copy of this superficially formidable document (running to about 550 foolscap pages, of which a fourth to a third is in the form of single-spaced footnotes and special appendices). Because of Dr. Temple's interest in my work, and since the circumstances of my personal traffic with the doctrine of the Trinity have been somewhat unusual, it seems fitting to include in this preface a concise summary of my studies and the influences predominantly connected with them. I embrace the opportunity to do so the more readily since I shall be enabled in this way to record a sense of debt to my last *Alma Mater*, the University of Oxford, that grows more quick and pregnant with the recession of the years.

It was as a student in the Episcopal Theological School, Cambridge, Massachusetts, about 1928, that I became immensely curious about the doctrine of the Trinity. This is the more unusual in that the major influences on my thinking soon became, and for a good while remained, the polemically turned researches of the late Dean Hastings Rashdall and the theological philosophy of the late Professor A. S. Pringle-Pattison. In the autumn of 1930 I went up to Oxford as Travelling Fellow of the Episcopal Theological School—an institution to which in many ways I am under a lasting obligation. For over two years I laboured hard at one subject, and one only, the being of God as Trinity and Unity. In particular, I began a serious firsthand investigation of the Patristic work on this doctrine, with the result that my thought and feeling with respect to the Trinity were revolutionized. I have been clear ever since that the foundation of any understanding or just appreciation of the doctrine of the Triune God is a thorough acquaintance with the Christian Fathers.

It had been my hope that some time I might publish a comprehensive, full-length work on the Trinity. Destiny has brought it about that the book that I had long visualized is instead a small volume with a partly devotional emphasis. I am, however, far from sure that there is not in this dispensation great gain, for there is no doctrine in relation to which devotion and adoration have always played, and will always play, a larger part than that of the Blessed Trinity. At the same time there has been no effort in the preparation of the present volume to minimize or play down the difficult intellectual issues involved. Rather our effort has been to keep in mind the fact that in the great ages of Christianity intellect and devotion, reason and faith, have been sworn allies engaged in a common enterprise, not adversaries desiring each to rule the other out. One cannot but think of St. Anselm of Canterbury, who was a monk before he was drafted to be an Archbishop, and who worked out the Ontological Argument for the existence of

God in a meditation itself addressed to God. Or, one remembers the extraordinary extent to which in all the varied writings of Anselm's philosopher successor, William Temple, there is an interfusion of thought and devotion. I imply no comparison with these illustrious names when I say that I have tried to treat seriously the doctrine of the Trinity as well as to bring out its crucial significance for Christian devotion and the Christian life, and indeed for human existence in our world. I simply anticipate an inevitable criticism—apart from whatever additional impediment an intense professorial experience may have contributed—of a work on this particular theme—namely, that the going is at times heavy. If it should be found to be otherwise, the author would convict himself immediately of a superficial, if not frivolous, treatment of the most profound of all subjects.

I am hopeful, notwithstanding, that many people without any training in theology or philosophy will read this book. I want to suggest, accordingly, that if any reader finds the going too stiff in Chapters I and II, he simply stop for the moment and turn to Chapter V. When he has finished it and Chapter VI, he will then be better equipped to read the preceding sections. The order of the book is right logically, but the application of principles makes as a rule for easier reading than discovering them and subjecting them to a thorough analysis. For this reason it may be wise for some readers to tamper with the order of logic.

I cannot attempt to list the scholars and theologians to whom I am indebted. The book will be eloquent enough in the unconscious as well as conscious and particularized proclamation of this debt. I do wish to take this opportunity to thank Dr. L. W. Grensted, Oriel Professor of the Philosophy of the Christian Religion at Oxford, for his guidance of my research in my Oxford period and his continuing interest and friendship. The Reverend Canon A. E. Baker, co-editor with the late Archbishop of Canterbury of this series of Lent Books, has helped me by his quick courtesy and his stimulating interest in the work proposed. I am under special obligation to my associate, the Reverend Craig E. Eder, who in the past few weeks and months has cheerfully shouldered an undue part of the Parish load. The

Vestry and Congregation of All Saints' Church, Chevy
Chase, have borne without complaint numerous pulpit
fugues on many of the themes of this book as well as some
pastoral neglect. To Mrs. Mary E. Cox, my former secre-
tary, who voluntarily undertook and has carried through
the onerous task of typing in triplicate a manuscript not
infrequently crabbed and irregular, I am deeply obliged.
Finally, without the encouragement and patience of my
wife, Edith Clark Lowry, I could hardly have finished the
task which is now complete. Through her criticism, also,
of the original manuscript some things at least are simpler
and clearer than they would otherwise be.

CHARLES W. LOWRY.

ALL SAINTS' RECTORY,
  St. Peter the Apostle,
    June 29, 1945.

CONTENTS

For we can do nothing against the truth, but for the truth.

ST. PAUL: 2 Corinthians.

By what understanding shall man comprehend God, when he comprehendeth not his very intellect, whereby he would fain comprehend Him? ST. AUGUSTINE.

Lord, I acknowledge and thank thee that thou hast created me in this thine image, in order that I may be mindful of thee, may conceive of thee, and love thee; but that image has been so consumed and wasted away by vices, and obscured by the smoke of wrong-doing, that it cannot achieve that for which it was made, except thou renew it, and create it anew. I do not endeavour, O Lord, to penetrate thy sublimity, for in no wise do I compare my understanding with that; but I long to understand in some degree thy truth, which my heart believes and loves. For I do not seek to understand that I may believe, but I believe in order to understand. For this also I believe—that unless I believed, I should not understand.

ST. ANSELM.

And chiefly Thou, O Spirit . . .
Instruct me, for Thou know'st; Thou from the first
Wast present, and, with mighty wings outspread,
Dove-like sat'st brooding on the vast Abyss,
And mad'st it pregnant: what in me is dark
Illumine, what is low raise and support.

JOHN MILTON: *Paradise Lost.*

CHAPTER I

Doctrine and Devotion (1)

OUR purpose in the following pages is to study a
particular Christian doctrine, the doctrine of the
Trinity, in relation to the life of devotion. The word
"doctrine" is related to "doctor." A doctor, in the original
sense of the word, is a teacher—a learned person who is
competent to teach.

An illustration is the long prayer immediately preceding
the laying on of hands in the ordination of a Priest according
to the use of the Book of Common Prayer.

> Who, after he had made perfect our redemption by his death, and
> was ascended into heaven, sent abroad into the world his Apostles,
> Prophets, Evangelists, *Doctors*, and Pastors.

The prayer is evidently based on Ephesians iv. 7-13, in the
English translations of which διδασκάλους is commonly
rendered "teachers."

This usage is still maintained, at least to a very great extent, in Great Britain. I well remember the curiosity with
which, when I had occasion to consult an English physician
or dentist, I noted that his nameplate invariably bore the
simple title "Mister." In the United States, on the other
hand, not only are physicians and dentists "Doctors," but
also, by popular consent, pharmacists and veterinaries.
There is a widespread feeling, also, shared by many of the
clergy themselves, that there is something slightly rude
about not calling a Protestant minister "Doctor." Whether
or not he has a Doctor's degree, honorary or otherwise, is
not as a rule a particularly relevant consideration. The
Episcopal Church is partly—but only partly—an exception
to this general tendency.

This phenomenon is perhaps related to the situation with
which our thinking must begin—namely, the decline in
modern times of concern with Christian doctrine. A doctrine is a teaching or view believed to be true. It involves
the intellect, for it is by reason that we think and use words
as the conveyers of ideas. This is as true in religion as it is in
physics or geology or medicine. Religion is not in itself

13

thought. It is a form of experience. It is primarily a sense or feeling or consciousness. It is the sense of the Holy or Divine as a great, mysterious and overpowering reality. It is a feeling of reverence in the presence of an infinite and eternal Being. It is the consciousness of God.

> I was only then
> Contented, when with bliss ineffable
> I felt the sentiment of Being spread
> O'er all that moves and all that seemeth still.
> . . . Wonder not
> If high the transport, great the joy I felt
> Communing in this sort through earth and heaven
> With every sort of creature, as it looked
> Toward the Uncreated with a countenance
> Of adoration, with an eye of love.

The poet Wordsworth may be open to criticism with respect to some aspects of his theology, but he was right psychologically in his understanding of religion and religious experience. Religion in its concreteness is basically a sentiment, a feeling, a sense. He who has not known "the spirit of religious love" has not come very close to experiencing religion.

This does not mean, however, that religion is simply feeling. Feeling is never isolated from other major aspects of the self as personal centre of activity and consciousness. It is associated actively and passively with the impetus to act or do which we call "willing." The will is the faculty or organ of conduct. Or, more accurately, the will is the self as a doer or active agent. It is the person mobilized for decision. Religion, for this reason, tends to issue in morality. It is never identical with morality. It is false to say with Matthew Arnold that it is three-fourths conduct. "Morality touched with emotion" is a singularly bad definition of religion. Yet the two things are inseparable, and this is pre-eminently true of Christianity, where the holiness or divinity of God is interpreted in terms that are drawn from human relations at their purest and most unselfish.

Nothing human, to be sure, is without some base alloy, some tincture or uncleanness. "If ye then, being evil," said Jesus, "know how to give good gifts unto your children, how much more shall your heavenly Father give the Holy

Spirit to them that ask Him."[1] In the relations of a good parent—a father or a mother—to his children we approach the maximum human virtue. We see, and may experience within ourselves, the greatest purity of which our nature is normally capable. In such relations love, unselfishness, longsuffering, patience, seeking not one's own, are realities. Forgiveness without limit is not unnatural.

It was for these reasons, no doubt, that Jesus Christ applied the name "Father" to the Divine Lord and King of the Universe, and proceeded to work out in parable and saying many of the implications of this for our thought of God and our feeling towards Him. The so-called story of the Prodigal Son is a case in point. But, as this story in fact illustrates most strikingly, such theology carries with it a revolutionary moral code. A large part of the New Testament is taken up with the development and illustration of this morality.

"Ye have heard that it was said, Thou shalt love thy neighbour, and hate thine enemy: but I say unto you, Love your enemies, and pray for them that persecute you; that ye may be the sons of your Father which is in heaven."[2] "Then came Peter, and said unto Him, Lord, how oft shall my brother sin against me, and I forgive him? Until seven times? Jesus saith unto him, I say not unto thee, Until seven times; but, Until seventy times seven."[3] The continuity of this teaching and the salient ethical pronouncements of St. Paul and St. John is striking. In St. Paul the concrete sayings of the Master are given an abstract and universal turn. This is the meaning of 1 Corinthians xiii., where in addition the thought of *agape* or *love* is so kindled by the Apostle's inspired imagination that his language rises to a lyric height unsurpassed in the prose writing of all the ages. Another example is St. Paul's statement in Romans xiii. that all the commandments are included in the saying, "Thou shalt love thy neighbour as thyself." "Love worketh no ill to his neighbour: therefore love is the fulfilling of the law." This passage is significantly a part of the epistle for the First Sunday in Advent. It is St. John, however, who combines the concreteness of Jesus with the generality of St. Paul and who at the same time shows

[1] Luke xi. 13.   [2] Matthew v. 43-45.   [3] Matthew xviii. 21-22.

most clearly the interrelation of morality and theology, of
code and creed. "Beloved, let us love one another: for love
is of God; and every one that loveth is born of God, and
knoweth God. He that loveth not knoweth not God; for
God is love."[1]

This passage, we said, shows the interconnection of
morality and theology. It is at the same time an expression
of the most profound religious feeling. Indeed, reversing
the whole trend of Greek philosophical theology, which
reached its climax in the view of God set forth in the
Metaphysics of Aristotle, it asserts that feeling or affection at
its deepest and highest is an element in the being of Deity.
Love is of the very nature of God. This conviction is the
mainspring of the Christian religion. It is the principal
reason for believing that God is in Himself a Trinity of
Persons as well as an ultimate and perfect Unity.

The immediately important thing, however, for us to
notice is that this passage from 1 John brings out the in-
separableness and coinherence (a trinitarian term) of intellect,
will, and feeling—of thought, act and emotion. As the will
is never operative apart from feeling, and as feeling is always
registered in some motion of the will, so the intellect is in-
separably related to both. Man is a thinker—always in some
measure. Ideas are an integral part of human nature—alike in
its structure and in its functioning. Nor are they simply pro-
ducts of the rationalization of feeling, desires, dynamic
urges, strong anterior motions of the will. They also "go
before" in the complex interplay of the various factors that
enter into the constitution and activity of the human psyche.
They are the stimuli of feeling, originally and also by way
of renewal and deepening. They are determiners of the
will.

Marxism is a capital illustration of the power of the idea.
It affirmed the omnipresence and the omnipotence of the
economic motive. Man, it said, lives by bread and by bread
alone. History is the story of economic determination. All
systems of ideas are *ideologies*—rationalizations of the one
dominating interest of mankind. Until the advent of the
prophet, Marx himself, these ideologies were the inventions
respectively of the several ruling classes of the various

[1] 1 John iv. 7-8.

principal eras of history. Philosophies and theologies were auxiliary aspects of the over-all complexes of ideas projected in different ages as a means of upholding the *status quo* and keeping in subjection the workers and producers of the world. After Marx they were revealed for the first time as effectual error, and their approaching demise was proclaimed. Marxian doctrine at the same time was heralded as a Gospel, as saving Truth, and was embodied in a missionary movement.

We have no desire to belittle Karl Marx. He was without doubt a genius, and history has begun to flow in new channels becasue of his thought and faith. Marx, Freud, and Einstein, someone has remarked, are the modern trinity of intellectual revolutionaries. It is remarkable that all three are members of the Jewish race. Nothing, however, is more certain than the inadequacy of Marxism both as a philosophy of history and as an account of human nature. It is, in fact, one of the great over-simplifications, one of the grotesque *tours de force*, in which the history of thought abounds. The sufficient proof of these statements is the analysis of the influence of Marxism It is as an idea, as a doctrine, as an absolute religiously conceived and preached, that it entered mightily into the stream of history. It is perhaps the most spectacular of all illustrations, next to primitive Christianity, of the truth of the dictum attributed to Victor Hugo: "There is nothing in the world so powerful as an idea whose time has come."

He would be a rash man who would predict the future of the Communist idea, embodied as it now is institutionally in the giant among the nations that is no longer asleep, Russia. It would be hazardous to prophesy the course or the duration of Marxist evolution. There is a close parallel, structurally and psychologically, between orthodox Communism and primitive Christianity. Both were at base eschatologies—that is, visions of a final order in which the existing evils of earth would be done away and the cosmos (nature and society) would be transformed. In Christianity the agent of salvation was the Messiah—Son of God, soon to return on the clouds of heaven. In Marxist Communism the translation was to be effected through the dictatorship of the proletariat. In each case Cæsar or the State was a

2

provisional, temporary necessity, living, however, on borrowed time.

What saved Christianity and made it the most nearly universal and the most fruitful of all religions was its capacity for development. It was able to assimilate to itself all the influential currents of the mind and drives of the spirit in Græco-Roman culture. Its greatest intellectual victory was the annexation of the Greek philosophical tradition, dominated by the outlook and many of the ideas of Plato. This led, it is true, to a loss of much in the Biblical view of God, man, and life that seems to us today most relevant to the issues of human existence. Marxism is one of the protests (from the Christian standpoint) that has driven the Church to a rediscovery of basic Biblical insights. It may be said to have compelled Christains to remember that He who quoted the ancient Scriptures, "Man does not live by bread alone," also taught His disciples to pray: "Give us day by day our daily bread." But what Christianity had that Marxism lacks was a transcendent God, independent of the world and unchanged by human subjectivity, a conviction that God Himself had entered into the world of space and time and matter and flesh and bread to show men not only in word, but in costly deed, that His inmost nature is Love, and an indwelling Holy Spirit of truth and charity and judgment.

Another name for these superlative possessions of Christianity, which as a matter of cold fact enabled it to survive and to bring to every subsequent crisis of its existence powerful resources, is the Trinity. What we are immediately concerned, however, to estimate is that the future of Marxism as such is highly problematical precisely because it is a religion of pure *immanence*, lacking the resources of humility, resistance to the demonic in the human soul, and a continuity of being that are inseparable from an inalienable core of transcendentalism.

But it is necessary now to leave the bypaths of illustration, entrancing and seductive as they are, and return to the thread of our sober argument in this chapter. Although religion is, in its primary essence as something that is experienced, a feeling, it is inseparable both from the will, by which man acts, and from the intellect, by which he conceives, thinks, and draws conclusions. In particular, man is a being who lives by ideas, thoughts, notions, formulated convictions, reasonings. If it were not so, his emotions would be those of an animal simply, and his will, his freedom, would be either the uncomplicated reflex of instinct or the registration in act of bare chance. History from the beginning until now is the proof that this is not the case. It is the saga of ideas as operative, creative, and destructive forces. Moreover, man knows within himself that no other account of his nature is possible. This is why the Greeks, who came as close as any people have ever come to freedom from illusion without the loss of humanity, insisted that man is a rational animal. Reason, they said, is the distinctively human attribute.

It was, of course, inevitable that man would exaggerate and distort the element of rationality in his make-up. He is a finite being, in part an animal, seldom in other than a state of imbalance. The motion of the physical universe, we are told, is by a series of jerks. Perfect gradualness is an illusion. This is true also of the mental and spiritual life of man. It proceeds by fits and starts. It is jerky, uneven, extreme in motion, "never continuing in one stay." So we get in the history of thought many "isms," usually expressive of exaggeration. We get idealism, materialism, intellectualism, voluntarism, pragmatism, vitalism, and so on.

Philosophy is in the main the story of a man attempting to be a pure reasoner. This attempt is bound to be in vain. The limitations of human reason are as evident as its reality and unescapableness as an element in man's nature. Plato, the greatest and the most fertile figure in the history of philosophy, knew this. Because of it, he had recourse deliberately to myth—to "the likely tale" that would come as close to conveying the ineffable and unknown reality as the mind could come. Later philosophers, including, on the whole, Plato's great pupil, Aristotle, were less cautious. Especially was this true of thinkers who undertook to make maps of reality after the breakdown of the mediæval synthesis and the separation into water-tight compartments of religion and philosophy.

This was the background of what the late Archbishop of Canterbury, Dr. William Temple, has so brilliantly characterized as "the Cartesian faux-pas"—the attempt, namely, to make reduction to clear and simple ideas the criterion of that which is real and the resultant sharp separation of mind and matter, soul and body, truth and myth, logic and life, thought and existence. Spinoza elaborated on a grandiose scale and with much less prudence and attention to "the reasonableness of common sense" the fundamental idea of Descartes. The result is one of the most imposing and admirable, and at the same time incredible and futile, of all metaphysical systems. The eighteenth century, the Age of Reason, was, as a whole, suspicious of vast and intricate philosophical structures. It was, however, even more naive in the degree to which it gave hospitality to "the sentiment of rationality." For the first time perhaps in human history it identified common sense with pure reason based (unconsciously) on mathematics. Against this background Kant attempted to stake out the boundaries of pure reason. If he bungled a task that was very necessary, he has the distinction of having dominated in one way or another virtually all subsequent thought — philosophical, religious and theological.

In addition to the effect of the "critiques" of Kant, the nineteenth century was under the spell of revolutionary discovery. It was a period of the opening up of vast new continents of knowledge, of the birth of new sciences, of the rise to supremacy of the inductive method. History as a science came into its own. Interest was centred on origins and on development and evolution. A *simply* abstract view of things and of being was no longer possible. Reality in its concreteness and complexity could no longer be denied. More and more general conclusions were arrived at, not by syllogistic logic or alleged intuitive certainty, but, in William James's phrase, were forged in the teeth of stubborn and irreducible facts.

There were two principal reactions in the world of philosophy. One was the birth of a new type of idealism. Reality was still held to be mental—that is, either a subject or an object of consciousness, a mind or minds and objects of thought. Since, however, in our consciousness the self or "I" must be an object as well as a functional subject before it realizes that it is conscious mind, the philosopher Hegel had the brilliant idea of preserving the concreteness and apparent being-for-itself of nature and history by interpreting both as the eternal Idea objectified—posited over against primal subjectivity as an other. Then, as in our minds in little, this otherness is overcome; the act of thought is brought to completion; in and through the creation or projection of the finite, God or the Absolute realizes His eternal selfhood in all its richness and plenitude. Such is Hegelianism in essential idea. An illustration which may make the drift of the position more clear is the story of the philosopher seeing Napoleon as he marched into Jena and remarking: "I have seen the Absolute on horseback." For Hegel the rational is the real, and the real rational; but ample allowance is made, so he thought, for the distinction between finite and infinite. Also the finite is not dismissed as mere appearance, but is vital for the very being of the Absolute.

The second reaction to the new pressure of empirical facts was materialism. It took several forms. There was the positivism of Comte. The word "positivism" is very instructive for understanding what modern science has done for the mentality of man. It denotes the view that the real is positive, tangible, manageable matter of fact—that which is the object of scientific research and technical mastery. Feuerbach was the German and Protestant counterpart of Comte, a Frenchman who was impressed by the ceremonies of the Roman Catholic Church and thought it a good idea to conserve them on a strictly "positive" basis. Feuerbach, like Marx, was a left-wing Hegelian. The latter, Marx, exactly inverted the system of the master. For dialectical idealism he substituted dialectical materialism, admitting the fact of ideas and their influence, but explaining them as by-products of matter.

There were other brands of materialism, as, for example, that of Haeckel in Germany and that of Buckle, Spencer and Huxley in England. With all these figures the influence of Darwin and his full-blown doctrine of evolution through chance variations and natural selection is direct and regulative. Spencer was the high priest of evolutionism. With an intellectual credulity and a moral hardihood unsurpassed in religious or other annals he elaborated a universal philosophy in terms of the positive fact of evolution.

Cramped as we are for space, one specimen of what he took as reason may be displayed for the instruction of the gentle reader living in 1946. "Progress is not an accident, but a necessity. What we call evil and immorality must disappear. It is certain that man must become perfect. . . . Always toward perfection is the mighty movement—towards a complete development and a more unmixed good." Buckle was fully as naive. The point to keep in mind is that faith in reason, the offspring of modern humanism emancipated from all classical Christian controls, was so powerful that it dominated materialism as completely as idealism. Modern science itself came to a maturity with an unexamined but actually quite undemonstrable faith in the universal uniformity of nature and absolute inviolability of natural law.

Today the picture is very different. Science itself has reached a sceptical period. It has discovered its ultimate limitations. It knows that the faith by which it was nourished for centuries is not certainty. Indeed, some important empirical evidence tells heavily against the dogma of the uniformity of nature, and there are scientists as well as logicians who affirm that natural laws so called are purely statistical. They are like the predictions of a life insurance firm with respect to the rate of civilian mortality in 1947.

In philosophy the dominant mood is one of radical empiricism, of determined realism. Idealism has few adherents, even in Oxford, which a Cambridge don once defined, in conversation with the present writer, as "the place where old worn-out German philosophies go to die." Many professional philosophers have given up any hope of a constructive metaphysic. Thought, they say, cannot move beyond the analysis and criticism of propositions dealing with the present matter of fact. Here we can see the lingering influence of nineteenth century positivism. Other philosophers decline to abandon reason altogether and seek to go behind both Kant and Descartes. They protest with Professor Whitehead against "the bifurcation of nature" and emphasize with the same distinguished thinker "the Fallacy of Misplaced Concreteness." By the last phrase is meant the view of positivists that science deals with concrete, factual reality. Actually, says Whitehead, the scientific method is one of abstraction. It has worked well. It has won "an almost miraculous series of triumphs." Its popular prestige is still enormous. But the fact remains that science operates by abstracting from the concreteness of actual event and actual being. It cannot help doing this. Even the simplest scheme of classification derogates at every point from the richness and uniqueness of the individual entities under observation. When philosophy fails to detect this, the result is disastrous. In a passage magnificent both as literature and as irony, Professor Whitehead indicts the main tradition of modern philosophy:

"These sensations are projected by the mind so as to clothe appropriate bodies in external nature. Thus the bodies are perceived as with qualities which in reality do not belong to them, qualities which in fact are purely the offspring of the mind. Thus nature gets credit which should in truth be reserved for ourselves: the rose for its scent: the nightingale for his song: and the sun for his radiance. The poets are entirely mistaken. They should address their lyrics to themselves, and should turn them into odes of self-congratulation on the excellency of the human mind. Nature is a dull affair, soundless, scentless, colourless; merely the hurrying of material, endlessly, meaninglessly."[1]

The exposure of "the Fallacy of Misplaced Concreteness" is one of the really brilliant and revolutionary intellectual achievements of our time. It is not less momentous for religion, the philosophy of religion, and Christian apologetics than for general philosophy. It serves as a warning also to theologians, though, as we shall see, Christian doctrine can never be fully abstract. It must bring into its formulation of Truth a large element of the concreteness of living religion.

If we turn from thought to the life of mankind, it is obvious that talk of "the flight from reason" is not prattle. War is organized madness, systematized and rationalized unreason. Modern science has brought about an improvement of organization and rationalization that would have seemed fantastic and incredible to our forefathers. Fascism is the supreme political expression of the instinctive and subconscious espousal in our time of unreason. Within the democracies this "wave" was more advanced than most liberals realized. France is an extreme case in point. The reaction of innumerable normal Englishmen and Americans to the new order in Italy and later in Germany was proof of

[1] *Science and the Modern World*, p. 80.

a notable sagging in liberal morale and ideology. This reaction was psychologically not different from that of the generality of leftists to things Russian from 1918 on. In the United States it is certain that many of the masses as well as the more privileged classes have lost the clear, regulative ideas set forth in the Declaration of Independence and embodied in the American Constitution. The recovery in thought, and in the moral consciousness that always underlies conduct, of "the sentiment of rationality" is the most urgent need of our time. Unless it occurs, and the world witnesses a new birth of freedom founded on an enlarged and mature reasonableness, the war will have been fought in vain and the future of mankind will be dark.

Yet such a prescription, obvious as it is, has in it an element of peril. Its understanding and application require careful thought. The very violence of the present storm is an indication that something was missing in what we may conveniently call liberal culture. That something was faith, God, a sense of fruitful contact with the unseen and elusive, ever transcendent, yet most real and powerful and compelling Mystery that undergirds and explains the universe. Reason was carried to an unreasonable and absurd extreme. It became the instrument of carnal pride, and the result has been a great disaster so that it is hardly too much to call it a second fall of man.

It is just here that the Christian religion occupies a unique position and has an unparalleled opportunity. Christianity stands or falls by the conviction that man has been created in the image of God. This means that the human intellect, as well as the human will and the highest human feeling, has a divine quality. It is like *in little* the mind of God. Religion requires a use of the intellect. It has progressed and become purer and deeper as reason has kept pace with and remained in fertile relationship with feeling and will. It is by the intellect that man has been able first to formulate and then to communicate and to deepen religious experience. This is the meaning and value of theology, of doctrine. Theology is the science of religious experience. Doctrine is the formulation in terms that are intelligible, and at the same time vivid and concrete and enkindling, of essential religious ideas.

This means that theology can never be the expression of pure reason. It can and should utilize the best attempts of philosophers to understand by reason man, the world and God. An example in ancient thought is Aristotle's proof of the existence of God and his portrayal in analogical terms of the being of Deity. The closest counterpart to this in contemporary philosophy is Whitehead's recourse on metaphysical grounds to God as the principle of concretion —that is, the ultimate entity or being without which there is no reason why creation should be at all. But theology knows the limitations of human reason. It knows that man is a creature. Further, he does not live by reason alone. He is a dynamic, a passional being. He lives by desire, by communion and community, by love and by hope. He is a religious animal. His supreme need is "the spirit of religious love."

Therefore theology, or religion become reflective, rejects in the name of a more mature rationality pure reason, cold logic, abstract thought. It is not entranced by "a ballet of bloodless categories." In formulating doctrines or cardinal articles of belief it is not afraid of symbol, analogy, myth. This is pre-eminently true of Christian theology. This theology has the longest experience in the history of religion of conscious wrestling with the problem of the relations of faith and reason. It embraces in its tradition the longest period of development and enlarging speculation incidental to continuous contact with the progressive secular culture. It is the most sophisticated of all theologies. Yet the Christian theologian knows better than anyone else the supremacy and the irreplaceableness of the historic Creeds as a formulation of the Christian religion. In these Creeds history, thought, poetry and mythology are intertwined and intermingled. The Apostles' Creed is the lyric of the Christian faith, breaking at the same time into narrative. The Nicene Creed is the Christian epic, stated in language that is Miltonic in the majesty of its inspired cadences.

Neither of these Creeds, unlike the later so-called Athanasian Creed, states explicitly the doctrine of the Trinity. The Apostles' Creed, rightly understood, implies it; and the Nicene Creed is intelligible only on the assumption that the one God of which it speaks at the outset is also in some sense three. But the doctrine of the Trinity is more scientific; it has in it more of a necessary inference, it is less concrete, it is less a reflex of immediate experience than anything in the Creeds or in the New Testament. Even so, it partakes of the preference of religion for symbol and analogy. It purports to give a picture of the God revealed in Christ— of the God of whom first-century Christians were to say without even an affectation of simplicity: "He is love." Such a conception of God in Himself, like the Incarnation in the Nicene Creed, can only be presented effectively and truly in the form of a myth—a picture or a drama or a story. Such a mode of presentation has on it necessarily the ear-marks of the finite. The infinite Being of God must be strictly inconceivable to us. But there is no other way in which to portray at all the nature of the God in whom reason and Christian faith together compel us to believe. The Father is God, Jesus Christ is God, the Holy Spirit is God. Here are three Divine Persons—faces or media of manifestation, and centres of consciousness. And since there is but one God, the Three must be so united as to constitute one Being. There are three Persons, but one God, one Lord. It is this God who has ever been and will ever continue to be the object of Christian worship and devotion.

A metaphysic which is pure, abstract, and entirely free from all mythology means the end of any living knowledge and a complete detachment from existence.

NICOLAS BERDYAEV: *Freedom and the Spirit*.

In Goethe, as well as in Kant, there was something cold—that belief in the absolute power and omnipotence of reason or the absoluteness of art! Kant's pure reason was an intellectual extract, an intellectual elixir—and hopeless. A purely rationalistic approach to life, to man and society, does violence to man, to his soul, and to all the human relationships, to family, to the inter-relation between parents and children, man and woman, brother and sister, friend and friend, to our social, political and communal associations, to our schools and colleges, and to any other realm of human civilization. Titanic rationalism of the German idealists not only ended in a fiasco, it ended in the gruesome catastrophe of the European continent. The Categorical Imperative did not save it. The Categorical Imperative, unchecked by the Lord of Love, ended in world destruction and in Wagnerian self-immolation. The road from Kant and Goethe to Stirner, Nietzsche, and Richard Wagner is not incomprehensible.

JOSEPH L. HROMADKA: *Doom and Resurrection*
(Discussing the views of T. G. Masaryk).

"Creator, nor created being, e'er,
My son," he thus began, "was without love,
Or natural, or the free spirit's growth,
Thou hast not that to learn."

DANTE: *Purgatory, Divine Comedy*.

CHAPTER II

Doctrine and Devotion (2)

THE word "doctrine" when used in a religious context has come to arouse deep suspicion. In spite of much stalwart defence of theology in Great Britain and in the United States of America, and in spite of the reversal within the past two decades of a long-prevailing anti-doctrinal trade wind in the Churches, the popular feeling has not changed. It is still supposed that doctrines are hoary concepts, moss-eaten with tradition, which spiritual and ethical religion left behind a long while ago.

Of all the Christian doctrines, that of the Trinity is perhaps the most suspect. It connotes not only a mystery, but one that is unnecessary. This point of view with respect to the Trinity arose as a conclusion of religious nationalism. It was very nearly universal among intellectuals in the eighteenth century. Thomas Jefferson, who has been aptly described as the "last great figure of the Renaissance," gave classic expression to the anti-Trinitarianism typical of the eighteenth century.

When we shall have done away with the incomprehensible jargon of the Trinitarian arithmetic, that three are one, and one is three; when we shall have knocked down the artificial scaffolding, reared to mask from view the simple structure of Jesus; when, in short, we shall have unlearned everything which has been taught since his day, and got back to the pure and simple doctrines he inculcated, we shall then be truly and worthily his disciples; and my opinion is that if nothing had ever been added to what flowed purely from his lips, the whole world would at this day have been Christian.[1]

The history of religious thought as of philosophical speculation is much more complex in the nineteenth century than in the eighteenth. For one thing the idea of development, the immediate antecedent of the full-blown doctrine of evolution, was discovered. It revolutionized philosophy in Hegel and theology in Newman. It brought in a totally new concept of history, exposing the static outlook of the older rationalism, in religion as in other matters, as illusory.

[1] From a letter to Timothy Pickering with regard to a sermon by the "Unitarian" Channing (who was actually an Arian), quoted by T. C. Hall, *The Religious Background of American Culture*, p. 172.

The romantic movement in literature, arising in the late eighteenth century as a reaction against stress on classical form and suppression of spontaneity and human simplicity, was soon at full tide. The Evangelical revival had acted even earlier to bring about a certain release of the springs of religious emotion. As a result feeling as an integral and powerful element in human life could no longer be ignored.

Yet the nineteenth century remained rationalist at heart. Indeed, we may say that in this century the impulse of rationality, freed from all bonds hitherto placed upon it in varying degrees by sober judgment and a sense of finitude or limitation, reaches the zenith of its age-long course as a dominant human motive. To illustrate, the nineteenth century rediscovered the reality and power of feeling. In religion it set feeling alongside reason and the moral will. But it witnessed no rediscovery of revelation as a category of experience and a basis of thought. Outside of Evangelicalism, increasingly a spent force, and Tractarianism, which in its genesis and first phases was stubbornly reactionary, the great forces were the ideas and emphases incarnate respectively in Kant, Schleiermacher and Hegel. All three thinkers were profoundly concerned with religion. They all assumed, furthermore, that Christianity was in some sense a final religion. They were unanimous, lastly, in being critical of the older type of rationalism as typified by Deism. Kant asserted the primacy of the moral will. Schleiermacher reduced religion to a carefully described and universally posited feeling of dependence upon, and oneness with, God or the Whole. Hegel held to reason: "the real is the rational, and the rational the real." But reason, in theory at least, was distinguished from the understanding or pure reason of Kant and was expanded to embrace all elements of human experience and all aspects of human culture.

See p. 90

Now the interesting thing is that all three thinkers and philosophers of religion were anti-doctrinal. Kant identified religion with the moral consciousness, and dismissed the doctrines of the Trinity and the Incarnation as both superfluous and inaccessible from the standpoint of human cognition. He is the closest in thought as in time to the rationalism of the Enlightenment. Yet paradoxically he attenuated all along the frontiers of thought the sway of reason and introduced into the very citadel of philosophy an ultimate and irreducible agnosticism.

Schleiermacher is the theologian of our triumvirate of thinkers. Turning from the study of philosophy and the philosophy of religion to Christian doctrine, he became "The Father of Modern Theology." Yet as one may speak in our time of the anti-scholastic scholasticism of a Karl Barth, what Schleiermacher really did was to eliminate Christian doctrine in the very process of setting it forth and expounding it from a new point of view. With respect to the doctrine of the Trinity, Sabellius he thought had been right. This doctrine is of value only as an intellectual reconstruction and summary of Christian experience. In fact, Schleiermacher is much more Sabellian than the real Sabellius, in all probability, ever dreamed of being.

Hegel, at first blush, seems to be an exception to the continuation within the nineteenth century of the anti-doctrinal wave of religious thought. He seems to be rather the reinstater of doctrine, for he was fascinated especially by the doctrine of the Trinity and did it the honour of adopting into his system a similitude of the Divine Trinity and making this the keystone of the ultimate cosmic arch which he took to be Absolute Spirit. But again appearances were deceptive. Hegel, in fact, discarded the orthodox doctrine of the Trinity along with the correlative ideas of the Divine transcendence and the Creation. For him all that is finite is an appearance of the Infinite. Process in all its phases is an integral and organic aspect of Absolute Mind. Later idealists of the absolutist variety simply dropped out any and all references to Trinitarianism. F. H. Bradley held that the God of religion, being by definition in relation to human spirits, could never be identified with the Absolute and all-comprehending Reality which is beyond all relations.

There were, of course, right-wing Hegelians who posited the compatibility of idealism and Christianity and took seriously the notion of the Trinity as a rational and philosophical ultimate. In the latter part of the nineteenth century, also, a new apologetic for the doctrine of the Trinity arose. The pivot of this apologetic was the idea of sociality and fellowship as involved in the *summum bonum* of human experience and constituting the goal of history. Of this type of Trinitarian thought we shall have more to say in a later chapter. Both revivals of the doctrine of the Trinity were unsuccessful either in stemming the anti-doctrinal tide coincident with the whole impact of the spirit of modernity or in resuscitating the ancient prestige of the dogma of the Trinity.

Nor is uncertainty about this doctrine confined to secular-minded folk of goodwill or to people who have largely given up Church and hope for little from it, but who assume still that they are deeply religious. Not a few clergymen and theologians, including some who are not extreme Modernists, have lost any real grip on the doctrine of the Trinity. I recall vividly a conversation some years ago on a celebrated street of Oxford with an eminent preacher and writer of the Church of England—a man who incidentally has broken several lances in defence of theology and has done yeoman service in the cause of English Christianity. Yet when I asked him what he had preached on the previous Sunday, it happening to have been Trinity Sunday, he replied: "Oh, I always preach on worship." On my putting in a word for the doctrine of the Trinity, he said: "I take it as frankly diagrammatic." Another divine—one of the most distinguished Nonconformist theologians then living —told me, also in Oxford, that Schleiermacher had been right: the only tenable position was Sabellianism.

This point of view is perhaps changing. To cite only three works. Dr. Nathaniel Micklem's *What is the Faith?*, published in 1936, contains one of the best-balanced and most thoroughly orthodox expositions of the doctrine of the Trinity to be found in English. In 1941 Miss Dorothy L. Sayers's brilliantly and originally Augustinian work, *The Mind of the Maker*, was published. Its theme is the trinitarian character of every creative work or act. Drawing upon her own experience as a creative writer, and analyzing from a similar standpoint many written works, Miss Sayers argues analogically that the God who has created the world and man must be both in Himself and in His activity a Trinity. Professor Leonard Hodgson in his *The Doctrine of the Trinity*, published in 1944, has advanced a radically Trinitarian interpretation of the Christian religion. The doctrine of the Trinity, which he sees as issuing necessarily, or even inherently, out of the Christian revelation, is put forward as in line with the empirical trend of recent philosophy. At the same time Professor Hodgson draws on idealism in an attempt to clarify and rationalize the idea that a plurality of personalities may be included and unified within a single personal life. The union in this work of religious sincerity, theological learning and philosophical capacity is noteworthy, and there can be no doubt that it will exert a wide influence.

Still we can hardly assume as yet even a substantial recovery of the conviction either that doctrines in general are necessary or that the doctrine of the Trinity in particular is essential to the Christian religion. It is expedient, accordingly, to examine afresh in the remainder of this chapter the nature of doctrine and its relation to devotion. In the next chapter we shall then go on to face the specific question of the relation of the doctrine of the Trinity to the Christian religion.

The word "doctrine" is used in a variety of contexts. Its employment is by no means a speciality of theologians. We read, for example, of the doctrine of entropy, sometimes called the second law of thermodynamics—the teaching, namely, that the nature of the physical universe is such that the energy of the world, from the standpoint of utility, is running down. Eventually the sun will grow cold, and the universe will become incapable of supporting anywhere life as we know it. Sir James Jeans has posited, on the basis of this doctrine, a view of the creation of the world strikingly reminiscent of orthodox Christianity. The Bishop of Birmingham, Dr. Barnes, has written that material for a new statement of the cosmological argument for the existence of God is afforded by the evidence of entropy, though he is reluctant on other grounds to use such an argument. Dean Inge, who, among other interesting traits, combines theological modernism with an intense dislike of philosophical modernists and their views, has used the doctrine in question as the groundwork of a brilliant refutation of the idea that God is wholly or organically immanent in the world.

3

Other scientific examples come to mind. One has heard eminent philosophers speak of the doctrine of gravitation, or of evolution, or of relativity. All three doctrines have become, and very likely will remain, dogmas in the technical sense of views or teachings accepted as authoritative. Here to a certain extent science recapitulates theology.

Illustrations from other fields could be added. In politics, for example, there is the Monroe doctrine and "the doctrine of the equality of all men" (Burke). Science, however, presents the closest parallel to religion. In both a doctrine is a view of the nature of reality in some aspect. Such a view is not arbitrary or a fancy. It is a formulation based upon evidence, a conception enforced by experiment or experience. It is an inference as to the character of that which is, required by certain facts.

A doctrine is, in turn, directive of present and future experience. It tends to be normative for the interpretation of new evidence. There is a presumption of essential continuity in the meaning of facts, given any particular area of experience and discovery. It is by assuming such continuity that science lives. The same thing is true of religion. "Therefore," said Jesus, "every scribe who hath been made a disciple to the kingdom of heaven is like unto a man that is a householder, which bringeth forth out of his treasure things new and old."[1]

The doctrine of evolution is a case in point. It is doubtful whether any other theory, or hypothesis, or description of reality in some phase, since the genesis of Christianity and the emergence of the doctrine that God is Love, has exercised an influence so epochal and revolutionary. Practically all fields of research and attempted understanding were drastically affected. Man's outlook on himself and his world underwent a profound transformation. Whether this was all for the good, and whether actually the universal extension of the doctrine of evolution as an interpretative concept was legitimate logically or empirically, is today open to serious question. It could even be argued that the virtual deification of evolution and the transition in our time from rational humanism to a dehumanization and debasement of human nature, unparalleled perhaps in

[1] Matthew xiii. 52.

all history, constitute a causal sequence. That, however, is not germane to our present argument. We are concerned to exemplify the nature and use of doctrine. Evolution will almost certainly remain a dogma of science, however much facts as a whole may require a trimming of its sails, and will continue to guide scientists in their approach to many areas of investigation as well as in the interpretation of their findings.

The function of doctrine in religion is very similar. The doctrine of Original Sin, for example, is a descriptive generalization. It is an account of the facts of human nature taken as a whole from a particular standpoint. It becomes a guide to understanding concrete human behaviour. Directed toward the jostling, tragic titanic stage of our historical period, it is like a searchlight cleaving the darkness. But it is no more an explanation of the facts of which it is a systematic account than evolution or gravitation or Freud's doctrine of the libido. In the end, of course, there is a great deal which men simply cannot explain. Reason can go, at best, only so far. This is the point of Professor Whitehead's dictum, as arresting and fertile as it is profound, that the existence of God is the ultimate irrationality.[1]

If science itself is far from being, in relation to pure reason, an eminent domain, with ultimate reality securely and reliably staked out and subject at every point to intellectual expropriation, religion has as its very province a realm of experience and discovery in which traffic with infinite and impenetrable mystery is the normal order of the day. This means that logic or pure reason is even less applicable as an exclusive methodology to the data of religion, and that its doctrinal formulations partake more evidently of symbolic and mythological expression. Pragmatically, this is momentous, for man is a believing animal; he is always as a whole moved more by feeling than by reason; and the whole crisis of our time is at base religious, having to do with the thirst of the modern human psyche, only in small part conscious, for a tenable and powerful myth.

This brings us to the subject of devotion in relation to religious doctrine, but, just because of the urgency of this issue for human existence in the twentieth century, it is

[1] *Op. cit.*, p. 257.

imperative to emphasize the essential reasonableness of facing and accepting the limits of pure reason. This is what Kant, the greatest philosopher of modernity, tried to do. It remains, even after all who have continued his enterprise, the most weighty unfinished business before the forum of the thinkers and seers of the world. Only as it is dealt with wisely and constructively is there hope of laying the spectres of unreason and madness that have brought mankind to the brink of the abyss. Here, too, is an opportunity without parallel for the Christian religion and the Christian Church. For Christianity is unique in the degree to which throughout its long history it has remained at once the champion and the critic of reason. In this respect it is the advocate and the exemplar of a final dialectic.

We turn now to the subject to which actually the discussion of doctrine has brought us—not arbitrarily or by any intruded manipulation of ideas—namely, devotion. Devotion has come to have a specifically religious connotation. We speak of books of devotion, of the devotional life, of private devotions. Indeed, it is for this reason that the present work bears the title that it does. There is, as we shall see eventually, a reason for this. High religion is, on its human side, in large part devotion or devotedness. It rapidly deteriorates, and tends to pass over into a species of sacred selfishness, as soon as the fire of personal devotion and love begins to burn low. This possibility explains a great deal in the history and in the psychology of religion in all ages and all places. It is the key to the alarming affinity that seems to exist between religion and respectability, piosity and mediocrity. It enables us to understand why self-centredness and genuine religious feeling—"a sense and taste for the Infinite"—can and frequently do co-exist in others and in ourselves. Only the answer to such possibilities and facts is not in pointing to extra-ecclesiastical respectabilities or to minor triumphs over inherent human selfishness without any obvious religious motivation. The answer is in understanding clearly the nature and psychology of human devotion, including its relation to religion at its highest, purest, richest and most inclusive. Such religion we believe is to be found in Christianity, and in Christianity alone.

In order to understand devotion we must begin, not with

religion but with psychology, not with philosophy but with experience. We must begin with man as he is. And we shall do well to keep before us a motto, not the resounding ancient words, "Man is the measure of all things," but the more sober and more authentically classical injunction: "The proper study of mankind is man."

The Greeks thought that man is differentiated from other created animals or animated beings (Aristotle applies to God the word ζῷον, from which "zoology" is derived) by the gift of intellect and reason. Bodily desires and passions the human being shares with the lower animals. In the *Phædo* Plato, speaking through Socrates, puts forward a point of view that seems very close to the doctrine of the Buddha as reported in the *Life* by Asvaghosha: "Therefore, again, all who are wise make this their aim—to seek a bodiless condition." Thus Socrates advocates as best the least possible intercourse between body and soul, not only because of the requirement of food by the latter and its liability to diseases, but because the body "fills us full of loves, and lusts, and fears, and fancies of all kinds and endless foolery." Even war is explained as due to bodily desires and demands. "Whence come wars, and fightings, and factions? whence but from the body and the lusts of the body?" Death is hailed not as an enemy or an evil, but as incalculable gain, since "then, and not till then, the soul will . . . exist in herself alone."

Such dualism is authentically Platonic, as it was presumably Socratic. Plato certainly never went back on the teaching of the *Phædo*. To understand, however, his whole outlook on man, one must take into account especially his view of *eros* or love as expounded in the *Symposium* and the *Phædrus*. The Plato of these dialogues is not a pure intellectualist. He knows that life, even of the soul, is not something inert and static. It is movement, attraction, innate direction toward an end. The mainspring of this motion, the primary urge or motive force of human being, is desire or love. It is *eros*. Only this desire is in essence spiritual; it is of the soul; it is aspiration toward ideal Beauty. This comes first; it is ultimate in man. Bodily desires and loves are distortions or shadows of spiritual love. The solution of the problem of life is the turning of the soul through knowledge, discipline and fair actions to the vision of eternal and absolute Beauty, which is one with the perfect and all-inclusive idea of the Good. If this Beauty is once seen, the soul cannot but be ravished by it, for such delight and ecstasy is man's true end.

The influence of what may fitly be called "the Platonic salvation" has been immense. The story of its total impact on Christian thought has yet to be written. Furthermore, the Platonic idea of *eros* contains much truth, which the powerful rediscovery in our day of *agape* (the New Testament word for love, not found as a noun in classic Greek) as a distinctive and unique form of love should not be allowed to displace. Of this we shall have more to say. Yet it is *agape*, or uncaused and unmeasured and freely outgoing Divine love, which really enkindles devotion. For love begets love. Sacrifice of self elicits a desire to offer self in return. The sublimated *eros* of the *Symposium* is lofty and sublime. It has an unending appeal to the ideal aspect of the human soul. But it remains remote and bloodless and impalpable. It is like the love of pure mathematics. Or perhaps it is like the ravished contemplation of such a mountain as the Jungfrau or the Matterhorn or Mt. Blanc, regarded as simply there and not as, with Coleridge in his great *Hymn*, a form of created existence in the universal praise of an infinite Creator. It will always be a highly aristocratic solution of the problem of *eros*, of doubtful validity for the average man and woman, and, it may be, hardly sufficient for the philosopher-king himself in those moments when he remembers that he is not a god, but a creature compounded also of flesh and spirit, desire and mind, dust and freedom.

The first great Christian psychologist was St. Augustine. He was a Platonist before he became a Christian, and he had absorbed and assimilated much of the Platonic intellectualism and spirituality. As a Christian, however, Augustine became a student, an exegete, and a preacher of the Old and New Testament Scriptures. The result was that he added, or rather prefixed, to the centrality of the intellect in God and man the primacy of the will. Man is a being who knows and loves, who has ideas and desires, who reasons and wills. These two basic motions of the human self are, however, not in harmony, for man has fallen away from God and from his creation in the Divine image. In consequence there is warfare between reason and the will. Indeed, the mind itself is involved in man's disorder and bondage of will. Reason, far from remaining free and competent, becomes the partial instrument and vassal of carnal pride.

The Augustinian analysis of the human predicament is thus more radical and inward than the Platonic. For Plato the crux is *reason and its ability* to see through and circumvent the senses. For St. Augustine the crux is *the will and its inability* to rescue itself and the personality as a whole from the bondage of pride and sensuality. Only God by the operation of His grace is able to remake the will and restore the balance of the self in its essential motions of reason and love. This God accomplishes both by directing the soul to the vision of eternal Mind in its perfection (the Platonic element in Augustine modified by Hebraic personalism) and by revealing His love and humility in Jesus Christ, God and man in one Person (the doctrine of the Incarnation, which Augustine emphasized was not to be found in Platonism). Either way the grace of God is distinguished from arbitrary fiat, although in his doctrine of predestination Augustine admitted a certain fateful element of ultimate arbitrariness and also of the primacy, by implication, of will over reason in God.

There have been various other efforts to isolate and throw into focus the essential attributes of man. Most of them are variants of the ideas of Plato and Augustine. In general the philosophical tradition has remained rationalistic. Whitehead remarks somewhere, with pardonable exaggeration for emphasis, that the most satisfactory general characterization of European philosophy is that it is a series of footnotes to Plato. In theology, from Duns Scotus (1308) on, the will has been the central problem. At the Reformation Luther directed against Erasmus and all Humanists his *Bondage of the Will*. Calvin rejected as a linguistic fudge the contention of Augustine against Pelagius that he did not deny freedom to the will. Jonathan Edwards in Colonial America followed suit, grounding his denial of the freedom of the will on the psychological analysis of John

Locke's *Essay Concerning Human Understanding*, studied assid-
uously by Edwards as a boy of fourteen in Yale College.
Anglicans or Episcopalians might do well, also, in this connection to re-read or read Article X in the back of the
Prayer Book.

In the nineteenth century, as not infrequently happens,
the pendulum swung to the opposite extreme and liberal
philosophers, theologians and divines came out unani-
mously for radical indeterminism or absolute freedom of
the will. James Martineau in England affirmed the existence in the self of "a liberty of indifference," as between
the claims of competing motives, prior to decision and act.
William James in the United States compared the freedom
of man in relation to the knowledge of God to the moves
of a novice in chess as opposed to the counter-strategy of a
master at the game. A distinguished living philosopher
once spoke in the classroom in the hearing of the present
writer of "the future as filled with the free deeds of men,
unknown even to God."

In our day a new approach to the essential character of
man has been made. It appears in some sense to go back to
the ideas of the "tremendous Dane," Sören Kierkegaard,
who after a century of obscurity has staged one of the most
spectacular intellectual "come-backs" in the history of
thought. It has been expounded by Heidegger, Scheler,
Tillich and Reinhold Niebuhr. Through the writings of
Niebuhr and the expositions of his pupils it has been widely
popularized at least in theological circles and more especially in theological seminaries. It is the idea of transcendence
applied to man as a whole—to his life, achievement and
consciousness. On this view man is essentially and without
any assignable limits a being who transcends himself—that
is, he has and is always exercising the ability to stand outside himself, his reason, his freedom, his cultural and social
fulfilments, even his provisional religious attachments and
securities. This is the explanation of man's infinite restless-
ness and insatiable appetency. It is the key to his seeming
inability to learn much from the lessons of the past. It is
the insight that illuminates the Christian doctrine of sin,
according to which sin is not primarily the voluntary com-
mission of specific acts that could have been avoided, but a

state and bias of the human being in his totality issuing with a fateful inevitableness in that worship of "the creature more than the Creator"[1] which is idolatry.

This sombre analysis of man, which at least has the merit of coolly facing and not trying to stare out of existence harsh and unpleasant facts, should not be confused with the conclusion of John Oman in his great book *The Natural and the Supernatural*. After noting that man has been defined as a rational animal, as a tool-using animal, as a laughing animal, and as a religious animal, Oman looks for a common root of all four characteristics. This root or stem he finds in man's supreme and dominating peculiarity—namely, that he has been able to gain a footing amid the varied flux of experience and casual circumstance, to resist the compulsion of the immediate, and to emerge the master and not the creature of environment. The reason for man's unique quality or capacity of transcending environment is found in the fact that he judges something to be sacred or of absolute value—not to be compared with ordinary goods or values. Otherwise there would have been, and could have been, no slipping of the leading strings of his nurse, Mother Nature, and man would have remained a simply natural being.

Oman's thesis, which is completed of course in the concept of a supernatural element in man's total environment, ever pressing upon man and leading him to faith and freedom, is not related to the attempt of emergent evolutionists and philosophical theologians indebted to them to define and describe spirit in terms of the capacity for apprehending and responding to absolute values. Spirit, it will be recalled, is the highest stage or step in the fourfold stairway of evolutionary advance, the earlier phases being matter, life and mind. One of the notable examples of such an approach to man and to God and the world as well is to be found in the writings of the late Archbishop of Canterbury, Dr. William Temple.

Against the background of all these insights, none of them certainly without an important element of truth, and in the light of man's historical existence as we are obliged to face it today, I wish to put forward the view that man is

[1] Romans i. 25.

in his essence a being who *loves and reasons*. Such a thesis must seem at first blush inordinately modest and unassuming. It may also appear inexcusably unoriginal. Yet the relation of what I want now to urge with the brief historical excursus just made will shortly be clear.

Man loves, and thinks, reasons, rationalizes—even investigates and generalizes from his facts with a fair degree of *transcendence* and objectivity—but only if the devotion and loyalty native to him have been rightly directed and firmly established. Otherwise he is at the mercy of false myths, unexistent gods, vainly imagined idols, and reverence for truth will go by the board. The most crucial and terrifying question of the present moment—from a purely sociological, political and national standpoint—is whether the epidemic of idolatry that followed upon the virtual demise of European *Christendom*[1] (excluding Great Britain), and found its most uncontrolled expression in Fascism, can be arrested and decisively beaten back. At this point politics and religion have been joined together by Fate for our generation, and no human power can put them asunder.

Of the two human basic attributes, love or desire is prior in origin and in the experience and development of the self. Mind is a comparatively late arrival on the scene, and, when it arrives, it finds that the will, to be defined initially as the point of impact and centre of registration for activity of the desires of the developing human person, has a formidable head-start. Further, love always retains its original priority. It remains in some form throughout a human life the mainspring of action. Reason may check it and refine it. It may re-enforce a nascent and partially effective self-mastery, which it should be the aim of nurture, education and religion to evoke and strengthen. It may partially inform and direct a concrete freedom of the will expressing itself in relative *transcendence* of competing motives, drives and desires. But reason never gains, at least with any security of tenure, the supremacy of the soul.

Such a view reverses rationalism alike in its Greek and in its modern idealistic expression. It is, however, by no means out of line with much that Plato saw and set down clearly with regard to human nature and behaviour in their con-

---

[1] Not Christianity.

creteness. It may claim to have squarely on its side the Christian religion, with its ancient realistic insight into the dynamism of men and even of angels. And it owes a great deal evidently to our two chief modern sources for the understanding of the human *psyche*, dynamic psychology and contemporary history.

Of these two sources, the first or modern depth psychology challenged early in the present century the claims of philosophical and religious rationalism. Instead of the integral rational image of man confidently and comfortingly held by leaders of thought for several centuries, the new psychologists developed the picture of man as a soul in contradiction. For, they said, underlying individual conscious mind there is a vast, adjacent, connected hinterland of unconscious psychic life. This hinterland is, as it were, a kind of park or preserve. In it there wander to and fro the desires, loves, anxieties and dooms which the conscious self, operating under a censorship which it did not establish, rejects or pushes aside. Thus the original "savage," revealed as far from "noble," lives on inside the civilized, moral, modern man.

For a time it was possible to ignore this analysis of human nature. Or, alternatively, it seemed possible to assimilate it as a moment in the evolutionary ascent of mankind. So powerful was the dogma of evolution and so strong the will to believe even in savants and scientists! Today such optimism is no longer possible. We know as a fact of historical existence that the crust of civilization is thin and that what we are pleased to call barbarism can spill over with a volcanic violence and brutality.

What made it possible for whole nations to surrender themselves body and soul to leaders and systems of doctrine and to plunge into a miasma of unreason, darkness and destruction? Was it some special disorder of collective soul or brand of national or racial wickedness? The answer cannot be a flat Yes, unless we are prepared to embrace in an inverted form National Socialist premises. It is of course true that nations like individuals have histories, and are at any point in their careers that which they have become through nature, experience, choice and fate. There were psychological predispositions and economic factors that played a prominent part in the genesis of the totalitarian state. Fundamentally, however, this powerful thrust of modern history, which not a few sincere liberals and Christians thought, and more feared, was "the wave of the future," came into being because men in vast numbers found life on an individualist and autonomous basis intolerable. They desired a satisfaction and a sense of meaning in existence which could be found only in union with something greater than self. Having lost the vision of God and the hope of immortal life in the fellowship of the Body of Christ, they deified all over again leaders, nations, races, places and natural vitalities. They immersed themselves selflessly, as devotees and idolaters, in the collectivities thus divinized.

But what of the pride and arrogance of man? What of his inborn and stubborn self-centredness? What of his will to power? Are these compatible with the theory that man is an inherently social animal, a being created for community, loyalty and love? The answer is clear if we analyze vanity or excessive self-esteem in any form. It could not exist without a social reference, without desire that is other-regarding as well as self-regarding. Pride would lose all meaning in absolute solitariness. Would a Henley have written an *Invictus* without the expectation of an audience? Would Nietzsche have troubled to pour out his soul in violent and calculatedly shocking prophecy if private self-expression had been his only motive? Would the strutting of a dictator have any meaning apart from the anticipated applause and adulation of surrounding multitudes?

All of which is not to say that reason is unimportant or its rôle in man's life a negligible one. Our whole purpose is to urge the contrary. But right reason demands that we "see life steadily and see it whole." It can only function fruitfully in relation to that which is, not in a vacuum of high abstractions or in an ivory tower of spiritualist illusion and pretension.

Man is will and intellect. His essential attributes are love and reason. By both he is differentiated from the rest of creation. Out of intelligence springs, no doubt, both the ability to fashion tools for use and a sense of humour. Also in time, as the mind develops, there emerges a capacity to form free ideas—ideas that transcend the flux of sense experience and the pressure of immediate desires. This is the foundation of the mental and spiritual life of humanity in all its aspects. Without it man would not be man. But the affectional or passional side of his being, which is sovereign at first in every human existence, does not retire from the scene. Neither does it cease to assert and strive for mastery in the ever-increasing complexity of experience. Rather it enlarges and increases in dynamic potentiality, partaking of and appropriating to its own uses the transcendence of sense and instinct which comes with the advent and growth of mind. It is in connection with imagination or the more or less free image-making power of the self, which is one of the outcomes of mind, that we can see most clearly the possibility of an indefinite expansion of the life of desire or love in the human being.

If reason is to be saved, along with natural love, it must be by meeting with an object great enough and powerful enough in its appeal to win the soul and gain its self-surrender and absolute devotion. The only object that can conceivably do this must be also a subject and must be Divine. It must be a loving God. And the love of God must not be a theory or a speculation; it must be a love that has shown its reality in sacrifice and agony, even when there was no claim upon it. Love must declare itself before it can be known to be love. The Word of God must go forth and become flesh and speak in clear accents to human hearts before men can believe in Divine love.

The prophetic and haunting words of Plato have lost none of their validity.

Very good, Socrates, said Simmias. . . . I feel myself how hard or rather impossible is the attainment of any certainty about questions such as these in the present life. And yet I should deem him a coward who did not prove what is said about them to the uttermost, or whose heart failed him before he had examined them on every side. For he should persevere until he has achieved one of two things: either he should discover, or be taught the truth about them; or, if this be impossible, I would have him take the best and most irrefragable of human theories, and let this be the raft upon which he sails through life—not without risk, as I admit, *if he cannot find some word of God which will more surely and safely carry him.*[1]

[1] Italics mine.

Only, in our time men have turned, as perhaps in his later years Plato did, to conscious myths. They have done so because, unable or unwilling to hear in Jesus Christ the Word of God, they have nevertheless felt within themselves a vacuum of spirit which reason, science, culture, humane progress, the sentiment of a universal enlightenment, could not satisfy. They have done so because man is inherently and unescapably an appetitive and devotional being—a being who is restless until he finds an object to which he can and must give himself in absolute loyalty and love.

The exposition and propagation of religious myths means doctrine. In National Socialism as in the earlier Communism, both of which were mythological in essential character as well as in the religious psychology engendered by them, there was no reticence and no nonsense about doctrine. Dogma was the order of the day, heresy was not tolerated, and the superior emotional impressionableness of tender years was exploited to the utmost limit. Said Lenin: "Give me five years' talk to the children, and my clock shall not be set back." And again: " 'Teach the children' is the meaning of statecraft always."

Christianity can never be as ruthlessly dogmatic as the great political religions of the first half of the twentieth century. To do so would be to do violence to its confidence that God is truth and to its respect for the freedom and sanctity of human personality. For Christianity to approach youth or age with an unqualified will to propagandize and to indoctrinate would be to stultify its very nature. Yet there can be no doubt that in their espousal of liberality and of the ideals of tolerance and universal private judgment the Reformed Churches (including the English Church and the Anglican Communion as a whole) have gone too far. The result is bound to be a swing to the opposite extreme, for authority of some kind the average person needs and will find somewhere. Freedom is a great privilege, and it is to be hoped that something of the high valuation of liberty characteristic of the eighteenth and nineteenth centuries may be recovered as a result of humanity's latest and most costly flirtation with tyranny. It is, however, far from certain that even a catastrophe as terrible as the Second World War will bring about a reversal of the deep shifting tides of human becoming.

Freedom is a privilege, but it is also a problem. Unconsciously, if not consciously, there is a desire in man, and sometimes a striving, to escape it. This is one reason why being a Christian is difficult, and it illuminates both the resistance of mankind to the Christian Gospel and the apparent compromises, from one angle, of the great authoritarian Churches.

The psychology of authority stands in a close relation to the understanding of man which we have set forth in this chapter. The ordinary and generally accepted idea of human freedom is a corollary of the view that man is to be defined as a rational animal. If, as we believe, man is predominantly an appetitive being, a creature who even in his rationality is ruled by love in some form, then the attribute of freedom is qualified by the impulse to surrender and obey. We have seen with our own eyes the power of this impulse. We have seen how demonic and frightening the will to give up freedom and to accept absolute authority can become. Yet totalitarianism as a sequel to liberal individualism is an event of history. It, too, is a witness to what is in man. This witness is that man is made not for solitariness but for community, not for an egocentricity that is necessarily half pretence but for the service in glad devotion of something greater and holier than self, not for isolation but for love.

Such a view is not against reason or opposed to a high valuation of freedom. Rather it is a statement of a truth that must be recognized and acted upon with the utmost seriousness and energy if reason is to revive her ancient reign and freedom is to exercise once more her former sway. But to begin with the notation that man is rational and self-determining is to put the cart before the horse; it is to start to run a steam locomotive with the coal car empty. Man lives by desire and valuation. He, too, as a creature is

by the Love impell'd,
That moves the sun in Heaven and all the stars.

His problem is not the generation of love. It is its direction and true orientation. It is meaningful encounter with a

Divine Lover in whom the needs and desires of man's disordered will can find satisfaction.

Does God exist? If so, what is the nature of the Divine? The first question is very interesting and very momentous. The second has in it the issues of life and death. The answer to it spells heaven or hell, hope or despair, joy or torment, peace or final unrest. It remains the question of questions.

For this reason Christianity may, and should, claim of all men a hearing. It is relevant at the point of the most intense hunger and thirst and suffering and wonder and terror of the human soul. It is a Gospel of Divine Love. It affirms that God so loved the world that He sent into it to live and die His only-begotten Son. It means by this language that God was so in Jesus Christ and in His passion and death that God Himself assumed and bore and overcame the sin and blindness and sorrow and tragedy of the whole world. Implicit in such statements are the doctrines of the Incarnation and the Atonement. You cannot affirm the truth of Christianity without these doctrines. They clarify and express at a certain point the fulness of the Christian religion.

But Christianity is even more. It asserts that God is in Himself love. His coming into the world as Lover and Saviour of men—as a Prometheus of history—was in no sense accidental or casual. It was not an arbitrary whim or a temporary ebullition of Divine magnanimity. It was an expression of the very nature of Deity, a temporal act manifesting his unchangeable and everlasting Being.

God came into history, God died upon a cross, God sent upon a little chosen band His own Spirit of love to bind them together and give them energy to shake and reshape the world. God did all this, because love and sacrifice and self-oblation and fellowship and unity in diversity are attributes of His essential and eternal nature. "God is love." The doctrine of the Trinity is the drawing out of this ultimate implication of the Christian Gospel. But we are anticipating the argument of Chapter IV as well as the one now to follow this attempt at expounding the meaning and the relations of doctrine and devotion.

A Will cannot be without a Word. A Will that is, and lives, must utter itself by a living Word.

FREDERICK DENISON MAURICE.

The Gospel story is a tree rooted in the familiar soil of time and sense; but its roots go down into the Abyss and its branches fill the Heavens; given to us in terms of a country in the Eastern Mediterranean no bigger than Wales . . . its range is universal; it is on the scale of eternity.

J. S. WHALE: *Christian Doctrine*.

Mid-numbered He in three of the thunder-throne!

GERARD MANLEY HOPKINS.

Where the self is no longer an autonomous subject, but is only the theatre; no longer speaking for itself, but only a sounding-board for God's utterance; where subjectivity is effaced by the truth, inasmuch as the latter does not merely permit itself to be apprehended, but itself apprehends: there takes place . . . the activity of the Holy Spirit.

EMIL BRUNNER: *The Philosophy of Religion*.

The Christian "story" may be told in an indefinite number of ways, but . . . it centres round three "mighty acts" of God—the creation, the Incarnation, the giving of the Holy Spirit. These three acts correspond not merely to three modes of our experience, but to three modes of the divine Being. Therefore the whole Christian story is epitomized in the triumphant declaration of the believing Church that Father, Son, and Holy Ghost together are worshipped and glorified, one God blessed for ever. Nor can any man deny this confession and accept the story which is the Gospel, the Christian revelation.

NATHANIEL MICKLEM: *What is the Faith?*

CHAPTER III

Is the Christian Religion a Trinitarian Religion?

THIS is the most important question that a theologian can ask. Theology, as we have already emphasized, presupposes religion. It could not exist in a meaningful way apart from faith. Faith is as essential for the Christian thinker as it is for the simplest believer. Frederick Denison Maurice, who I believe deserves to be called the Augustine of Anglicanism, considered it one of the inestimable values of the Apostles' Creed that it preserved Christianity for children and peasants and prevented philosophers from reducing the religion of Christ to abstractions suitable for them but not for mankind as a whole. We may, I think, looking at things almost exactly a century later than Maurice, modify this judgment and urge with a good deal of confidence that the Christian creeds are vitally important to the thinker precisely because he, too, must "believe in order to know." He is at this point exactly on a level with the peasant. Real Christianity means faith. The "I believe" of its creeds for ever separates it from any philosophy of religion or system of self-evident ideas. But this means that the question, What is the Christian religion? is one that matters desperately. If you are going to stake your life on the integrity of a friend, you want to know as clearly as you can the kind of person your friend is.

We have spoken of peasants and philosophers and of their respective relations to faith and the nature of religion. The same issue is obviously no less momentous for the typical religiously-minded person of our liberal, democratic culture—the person who in some way and in some degree lives by values that transcend egoism and self-centredness, and who feels within his soul a sense of awe and reverence for values, powers and mysteries that are greater than himself or any social group. This is good so far as it goes. Such a person may well have his feet upon the threshold of the Kingdom of God. But it is not enough to be a seeker after God in a vague and general way. Religion means truth. It is concerned with the factual and the real. Truth is as important in the life of the spirit as it is in the enterprises of

the intellect. And it demands in both ardent search and
single-minded devotion. It never comes as the reward
either of pure passivity or of vacillating half-heartedness.

Is it possible to attain religious truth? In one sense it is
harder to come at than truth in other areas of experience.
The concern of religion is with the unseen and eternal.
True religion is "fellowship with the infinite mystery."
No one has had the experience of seeing and understanding
in a clear and communicable way this mystery. Even the
mystics, who by definition are religious men and women
that have had the experience of immediate contact and
union with God, have insisted that their knowledge was
not that which could be put into words. In the phrases of
William James, the mystical experience is *noetic* but *ineffable*. The testimony of Biblical religion is the same. "No
man hath seen God at any time."[1] "For now we see through
a glass, darkly."[2] "For we walk by faith, not by sight."[3]
"The blessed and only Potentate, the King of kings, and
Lord of lords; who only hath immortality, dwelling in
light unapproachable; whom no man hath seen, nor can
see: to whom honour be and power eternal."[4]

Science, by contrast, measures. It sets out from the data
of sense perception. Such data are public matters of fact.
We might say conveniently that the realm in which science
ordinarily works is specified by St. Paul's phrase: "the
things which are seen."[5] Yet the odd thing is that modern
theoretical science ends in the same epistemological dilemma
that the most abstract theologian does. For the scientist,
too, all things go out in a mystery. He does not know the
ultimate nature of the material realities with which he deals
so familiarly. He cannot establish certainly the truth of the
assumption on which the whole structure of modern science
has been built—namely, the uniformity of nature or the inviolability of natural law. His empirical gnosticism fades
into a symbolic agnosticism.

Similarly theology, which is the science of religious experience, is compelled in the end to have recourse to
analogy and symbol and to acknowledge that here, too,

[1] John i. 18; 1 John iv. 12.   [2] 2 Corinthians xiii. 12.
[3] 2 Corinthians v. 7.   [4] 1 Timothy vi. 15-16.
[5] 2 Corinthians iv. 18.

man's "reach" exceeds his "grasp." But in the religious quest for truth humility and empiricism are as requisite in all stages of the journey as they are in other avenues of human exploration and endeavour. "Sit down before the facts as a little child," said Huxley the scientist. Few more reverent or more Christian statements were uttered in the nineteenth century.

The Christian religion claims to embody and witness to ultimate truth. It puts before men as Lord, King, Saviour, and Example an historic person who said, "I am the Truth." It speaks of a Divine or Holy Spirit as being "the Spirit of Truth." Going behind both—the visible Person and the invisible Spirit—and pointing to the ultimate power, authority, and source of all, it speaks of an eternal Father, unchangeable in character, of infinite knowledge, wisdom and love. "There is," begins Article I of the Anglican *Articles of Religion*, "but one living and true God."

If this claim of Christianity to point to the Truth—to present a clear and final answer to the question uttered by Pontius Pilate on his judgment seat—is well founded, or if the evidence so far as we can go is sure and strong, then the religiously-minded person must attend to the Christian facts. He must submit himself to them, let them make their own impression, and then conclude and act in accordance with what he finds. It is facts which are wanted.

This point has been put by Miss Dorothy Sayers in a passage that is assured of a hearing once it is begun, because of the combination in it of conviction, aggressiveness in the attack, and a liberal dose of the most serious and damaging of all forms of humour—namely, satire.

"Volumes of angry controversy," writes Miss Sayers, "have been poured out about the Christian Creeds, under the impression that they represent, not statements of fact, but arbitrary edicts. The conditions of salvation, for instance, are discussed as though they were conditions for membership in some fantastic club like the Red-Headed League. They do not purport to be anything of the kind. Rightly or wrongly, they purport to be necessary conditions based on the facts of human nature. We are accustomed to find conditions attached to human undertakings, some of which are arbitrary and some not. A regulation that allowed a cook to make omelettes only on condition of first putting on a top hat might conceivably be given the force of law, and penalties might be inflicted for disobedience; but the condition would remain arbitrary and irrational. The law that omelettes can be made only on condition that there shall be a preliminary breaking of eggs is one with which we are sadly familiar. The efforts of idealists to make omelettes without observing that condition are foredoomed to failure by the nature of things. The Christian Creeds are too frequently assumed to be in the top-hat category; this is an error; they belong to the category of egg-breaking. . . . The necessary condition for assessing the value of creeds is that we should fully understand that they claim to be, not idealistic fancies, not arbitrary codes, not abstractions irrelevant to human life and thought, but statements of fact about the universe as we know it."[1]

Miss Sayers outlines in these provocative sentences her own focus of approach to the nature of the world and the being of God. She is interested in examining man in his rôle of creative artist and in surveying critically his work. By implication she outlines an empirical approach to Christian theology of a vast and far-flung scope. In the main this is the right attack. If there are problems of methodology (science of method) and epistemology (science of knowing) that are complex and that the honest theologian must deal with in a manner that is less simple than Miss Sayers apparently envisages, this is not a matter for surprise. How many theologians have mastered the complexities along with the fundamental and scarcely varying simplicities of writing detective fiction?

It is beyond the scope of this book to examine philosophically the Christian religion, or in any way attempt to prove by recourse to all available facts of history and experience its truth. We are not interested in advancing a judgment as to how far such proof would be possible, and, if possible, of what value it would be. What we do want to point to in this chapter, and to drive home emphatically and insistently, is the fact that Christianity has been from the beginning a Trinitarian religion. Furthermore, if it were to lose its historic trinal character; if it were to be regarded, as by the rationalists of the eighteenth century, as the simple publication of self-evident and immutable truths; or if it were to be reduced, as by many later disciples of a prolonged but actually waning Enlightenment, to the universal truths, accidentally enunciated by Jesus since He certainly said a great deal more, of the Fatherhood of God, the infi-

[1] *The Mind of the Maker*, pp. 15-17.

nite value of the Human Soul, the Brotherhood of Man, Salvation by Character, and the rest, it would be a new religion. It would not be the Christianity of the Apostles and Prophets, of the Christian Fathers, of the mediæval doctors, of the Protestant reformers, of the great Anglican divines, of the saints and martyrs and missionaries of the Holy Catholic Church in all ages. It would not be the faith of the New Testament and of the great central tradition of the Church down to the present hour. The primary doctrines of the Incarnation, the Atonement, Grace, the Holy Spirit, and the Church would lose their logical ground and the abiding source of their power. The doctrine of the Trinity is the one all-comprehensive Christian doctrine. It gathers up into the seam of a single grand generalization with respect to the being and activity of God all the major aspects of Christian truth. It is the formulation which the Christian facts in their totality compel.

This has been the consciousness of the Christian Church from a very early time. Some Modernists have made much of the fact that, according to the evidence of the Book of *Acts*, Baptism was originally administered simply in the name of the Lord Jesus. In reality, this makes more remarkable and impressive the equally indisputable fact that by about A.D. 85 in the Gospel, which by general consent is the most nearly official and authoritative Church document of the first century, the concluding words contain the unqualified injunction, sent forth as a command of the risen Lord Himself:

Go ye therefore, and make disciples of all the nations, baptizing them into the name of the Father, and of the Son, and of the Holy Spirit.[1]

The phrase "into the name" does not correspond, as Harnack and others have noted, to any familiar Greek mode of expression. It is a very Jewish phrase. The Evangelist who set it down must have been aware of this and of its parallelism with the holy, reverend, and "awe-full" name of the Lord, Jehovah. He must have been equally aware of the sharp break with Judaism represented by including under a singular name not simply the Father,

[1] Matthew xxviii. 19.

with the Jewish as well as Christian associations of such a
term, but the Son and the Holy Spirit. When we note,
finally, that he could hardly have been unconscious of the
associations for all Jews of the "Name" with the ancient
Shema:

> Hear, O Israel: Jehovah our God is one Jehovah,[1]

we are compelled to see in St. Matthew's Trinitarian formula for Baptism one of the most arresting and humanly
inexplicable phenomena of primitive Christianity.

Modern critical scholarship has paid, I believe, insufficient
attention to Matthean Trinitarianism. Modern theology
has too lamely, in this as in other matters, accepted the
lead of specialized Biblical "scientists," not realizing that
these gentlemen (for whom I have in general high respect
and in some instances affectionate regard and gratitude)
are also human beings and find objectivity and freedom
from anteriorly conceived controlling presuppositions no
less difficult to achieve than the rest of us. The only tenable
explanation of St. Matthew's Baptismal formula is that at
the time of the writing of this "official" Gospel—somewhere around A.D. 85—the Church, as represented at least
by a very influential section of it, believed that the crucified
and risen Son of God and the Spirit of the Lord were *both*
distinct entities or "Persons" *and* at the same time united
in some very close way with the Father-God of Israel and
the Master's own teaching, and sharing in the heavenly
glory and universal authority of the Lord of Sabaoth. "All
authority is given unto Me."[2] Or, more simply, the believing and worshipping Church of A.D. 85 looked in thanksgiving and trust and expectation to Three in the highest
heaven—not simply to One. At the same time there was,
they knew, a perfect unity of will, thought and action as
among the Three, and there was, they must have assumed
(though here we can only speculate), some kind of ultimate
common Divine Being, since the Son certainly was of His
Father and the Spirit was the cosmically operative breath
of the Lord Jehovah. At any rate there was in this Trinity
none of the personal dissonance, active spiritual divergence,
and conflict of will characteristic of the many gods of pagan-

---

[1] Deuteronomy vi. 4.   [2] Matthew xxviii. 18.

ism. And the idea of a single Divine name was retained. After all, the early Christians were with few exceptions born Jews. If they were not sure about all the implications of the faith they had embraced in addition to that of the Synagogue, that is hardly a cause for surprise. It was not the first time that men have acted with courageous decision and found themselves in possession of a prize of rare and marvellous beauty, and yet have found themselves incompletely sure as to the reasons for their audacity.

The subsequent history of the Church is the history of the maintenance and the development of the same consciousness. The new element, as influential as it was complicating, was the rejection of Christ by Israel and the transplantation of the Church to Gentile soil. An accompaniment of this was the inheritance by the Church of Greek philosophy and the relegation to Gentile Christian minds of the task of thinking through the intellectual problem of the Trinity. To this task were brought all available categories derived from the greatest thinkers of Greece and the speculative subtlety and boldness that was as native to the Greek intellect as it was foreign to Hebraism.

The result was much intellectual experimentation and vast confusion for, roughly, two and a quarter centuries—the period known in history books as the Ante-Nicene Age. The controlling interpretative concept was that of the *Logos* or rational Word uttered or put forth as a kind of emancipation from the Divine mind with a view to the creation of the cosmos. This concept is generally thought of as Greek, and it is Greek in respect of the emphasis upon rationality both in God and in the order of the world brought into existence. But the dynamic element in it, the idea of a creative act involving a putting forth of power, is Hebraic. It goes back to "the Word of the Lord" of the Old Testament. It was from these Scriptures of his people that the Alexandrian, Philo Judæus, the real founder of Logos Theology, derived the notion of a creative Word; and it was as a religious philosopher, a believer seeking to understand, that he undertook the task of expounding the Old Testament Word in terms of the Greek *Logos* or reason.

It is unnecessary to go into the details of Philo's exposition. It is sufficient to note that he adopted the Greek view of the Divine transcendence according to which God as pure or perfect being cannot be thought of as having direct and unmediated contact with the world, and that he called the Logos or creative rational Word projected from the Father "a second God,"[1] in order to bring out the latter's subordinate and mediatorial status. This phrase, which had in it the seed of Arianism, caused the Ante-Nicene Fathers immense trouble.

History, however, like life itself, proceeds by trial and error, and many lessons were learned in the two hundred years before the Council of Nicea. Some of these were negative. Others were positive and of lasting value, such as Tertullian's use of the words "person" (*persona*) and "substance" (*substantia*), and Origen's doctrine of the eternal or timeless generation of the Son. Also here and there, especially in the West, there was a recovery of the Biblical idea of Divine transcendence, according to which God is at once in His unique and perfect being other than the world and yet able to act upon and within the world. Accordingly, when the Arian controversy burst like a flood upon the Church and the world (for under Constantine Christianity had been made the religion of the Roman Empire), there were ample resources of insight and intelligence to meet it.

In the West Arianism was never a threat. At the first General Council in A.D. 325, convoked by Constantine himself, fresh from residence in the West, there was no great difficulty in drawing up a Creed that repudiated and proscribed the Arian position in no uncertain terms. The original Nicene Creed was, in fact, a far stiffer and less lenient statement than "the Creed commonly called the Nicene" of the Book of Common Prayer—a formulary that with a few minor changes goes back to the year 374 and began not long thereafter to replace the older summary of the Faith in popular esteem and liturgical use. The later Creed, in addition to allowing more latitude of interpretation, is a much richer and fuller Confession, for in 325 the Bishops were content to end the Creed proper with the words: "We believe also in the Holy Spirit." Failure for centuries to make much of the work and Person of the

---

[1] δεύτερος θεός.

Holy Spirit was one of the bad fruits of the rationalistic bias imparted to nascent Christian theology by the Greek spirit and the early predominance of the Logos doctrine.

In the East the situation was serious for two reasons. First, the great majority of Eastern Bishops and theologians were Arians or quasi-Arians. The Nicene Rule of Faith was regarded as a high-handed innovation. Second, the Emperor Constantine, who as sole ruler had now changed the imperial seat to the East, came under the influence of an arch-Arian, Eusebius of Nicomedia. It was this Bishop Eusebius who managed (he had of course signed the Nicene Creed and may have entirely deceived the Emperor) to succeed the venerable Hosius of Cordova (Spain) as Chief Court Chaplain, and who officiated at Constantine's baptism on his death-bed. Furthermore, the children of Constantine and his nephew, the melancholy and ill-fated Julian "the Apostate," seem to have been given Arians as tutors, thanks to the same Eusebius.

This was the background of the real epic of the Arian conflict, which was the struggle of St. Athanasius almost single-handed to stem the tide of false belief. It was his gallant and ultimately successful battle that gave rise to the legend: *Athanasius contra mundum* (Athanasius against the world). In this battle, also, issues were raised and clarified in such a way that Christian theology, and through it also the Christian religion, came to full self-consciousness.

Let us set down very simply these issues. Arianism set out from the essential aloneness and aloofness of God. Here we have to do with the Greek philosophical notion of Divine transcendence, given a more personalist and anthropomorphic turn. The Arian theology might indeed be said to contain an ingredient of anticipated Mohammedanism. God is the All-great, the All-good, the All-powerful, but He is shut up in eternal inaccessibility. It is of His Divine essence that His perfection is something incommunicable and utterly apart.

The world, accordingly, is not created by Almighty God in any direct sense. It is created by a subordinate being called into existence out of nothing and called "Son" and "Word" and "the Firstborn of all creatures." (Here Arius and his disciples could and did cite Colossians i. 15 and

caused Athanasius a great deal of trouble.) This great demigod in time willed to be made flesh, and was born and lived
on earth as Jesus Christ. The Incarnation was no problem
intellectually to Arius, since the pre-existent Son was Himself a creature with free will, and therefore mutable and in
process of going on to perfection. No question of a human
soul, mind or will arose.

The purpose of the Incarnation of the Word seems to
have been, in Arius's mind, to give to us men a perfect
example, and thus to influence and lead us to a right use of
our creaturely free will, and thence to an achievement of
immortal destiny, reversing the fate of our first ancestor,
Adam. There is, I believe, little doubt that the ultimate
source of Arianism was Antioch, which in the middle and
late third century was the seat of a theological seminary
(or college) that emphasized literalism in the exegesis of
the Bible and preferred the *Ethics* of Aristotle to the Socratic
wisdom of Plato. Perhaps also the *Metaphysics* of Aristotle
(which contains his theology) was highly valued, although
this is only a guess.

What Arius did (whether it was something original or
simply what he absorbed from his theological teacher at
Antioch, Lucian) was to take both Biblical literalism and
Aristotelian ethics very seriously. The transcendental
theology was accepted in some form by nearly everyone
anyway; so the question of its source is unimportant.
Arius put everything together with a flawless logicality,
and brought forth the system that entranced the Alexan-
drians so much that he became a down-town preacher of
immense popularity and nuggets of his theology were
thrown into the form of *Thalia* or drinking songs and were
often to be heard as boatmen plied their way up and down
the Nile.

To this view of Christianity in all shades and degrees
Athanasius of Alexandria, the Deacon who, in response to
popular clamour, was made a Bishop at the age of thirty
without ever having been ordained Priest, uttered one of
the mightiest "Nays" of history. He said: "They shall not
pass," and in resisting the enemy cheerfully embraced
"blood, sweat and tears" and a more or less continual
threat of violent death. His reasons were intuitive rather

than ratiocinative; they were in terms of insight and practical reason rather than of systematic coherence, at least on one level, and unassailable syllogistic logic. He saw that, although Arius might have saved the letter of the New Testament at many points, he had entirely lost the spirit. He discerned that Arianism meant the loss of redemption, a false humanism, the reintroduction of a polytheistic paganism, and the destruction of the very idea of Divine love and sacrifice—the fundament and crux of Christianity as a religion.

So against the doctrines of the Arians Athanasius opposed the theses that the Word was of the very essence or being of the Father, His proper offspring or Son in whom dwelt the whole richness and plenitude of Godhead; that it was this Word, perfectly one with the Father and yet not to be confused with Him, who was made flesh in Jesus Christ; that God Himself, the Being of beings, had entered into human history in a human form, to unite manhood with Godhead and as man to meet and vanquish Satan, Sin and Death; that God, though in a sense plural, was essentially and absolutely one, as the Old and New Testament Scriptures so clearly taught; and that not one Divine person, but all three, the Triad or Trinity itself, was the Creator of the world.

St. Athanasius was not a great philosopher or an especially brilliant intellect. He gave the world no creative system. He is not always clear or consistent or completely cogent in his arguments and expositions. He bequeathed to his successors many unsolved problems of theology. But he knew what he believed; he saw deeply and surely into fundamental issues; he both valued logic and recognized its limitations; his ability to come to the main point and then never let go amounted to genius. In consequence, Athanasius saved Christianity in the East. He did even more. Through him the Christian religion became aware of itself in a new way. It reached a new and decisively important stage in its development and approach to maturity as an historical religion.

This stage is embodied for all time in the second paragraph of the Nicene Creed (we need no longer trouble to reserve to the Creed of 325 this designation; the Creed put

into the Book of Common Prayer is to all practical intents
and purposes the Nicene Creed). The main point of this
paragraph is to affirm the central conviction of Athanasius,
shared by his predecessor Bishop Alexander of Alexandria
and innumerable Christians of West and East, but grasped
and expounded with peculiar clarity by the Deacon, Bishop
and saint who was not afraid of martyrdom and not afraid
to stand against the world. This conviction is that in Jesus
Christ, in His life and sacrificial death, in His whole human
historical existence, we have to do, not with a man among
men, not with an angel of mercy and peace, not with a
great demigod, one among many mighty powers of the
universe, but with God, the highest God, the Almighty
God, the only God there is. To express this and to leave
us in no doubt as to this meaning the Creed says: "Very
(or true) God"; "Begotten, not made" (as we, finite creatures, are made); "Being of one substance with the Father"
(an awkward translation of words which mean "of the same
identical being or reality as the Father"); "Who for us men
and for our salvation came down from heaven," etc.

Here we have the first step in the Trinitarian logic,
which is a logic derived from experience, not speculation.
Here in the Nicene Creed is the absolutely definite, clear
crystallization of the fact that led necessarily and irrevocably
to a new conception of God and to a radical revision of
man's understanding of the Divine Being and the Divine
life.

The fact is, of course, writ large in the New Testament.
"God was in Christ reconciling the world unto Himself."[1]
"And the Word was God."[2] "Who being the effulgence of
His glory, and the exact image of His substance."[3] "For in
Him dwelleth all the fulness of the Godhead bodily."[4]
"He that hath seen Me hath seen the Father."[5] "And now,
Father, glorify Thou Me with the glory which I had with
Thee before the world was."[6] The import and the implica-
tion of these statements are clear. It was on such passages,
along with the general consideration that the integrity of
the Christian revelation hangs on the question of the ulti-
mate being of Jesus Christ, that Athanasius rested his case.

---

[1] 2 Corinthians v. 19.   [2] John i. 1.   [3] Hebrews i. 3.
[4] Colossians ii. 9.   [5] John xiv. 9.   [6] John xvii. 5.

The situation has not changed in any essential respect. Christian thought today has either to base itself on the Athanasian position or go back to the beginning and work out something like Arianism or simple adoptianism. Adoptianism—compare "adopting a son"—is the ancient and modern heresy that Jesus, a man born of Mary, so pleased His Father in heaven by the right use of His free will that the latter named Him "Son" and elevated Him to a position of unique honour and authority. The only real difference between Arianism and adoptianism is that Arianism was more "Fundamentalist": it tried to do justice to the Pauline and Johannine doctrine of the pre-existence of Christ (that is, His existence in heaven prior to His birth as a human being). But as regards thought about God and man and sin and salvation, the two alternative reconstructions of Christianity issue logically in much the same position.

This brings us face to face with the problem of the New Testament, and indeed of the Bible as a whole, in relation to the idea of Divine revelation and the truth of the Christian Gospel. No issue is more critical for Christianity in our world, and no issue is evaded so habitually in the generality of recent and current theological and religious works. This is the more remarkable and serious in view of the revival of the classical distinction between revelation and reason and the widespread tendency even in Anglicanism to accentuate the former as a unique and irreducible category.

To cite a conspicuous example, Professor Leonard Hodgson, speaking of St. Thomas Aquinas's view that the Trinity is a revealed doctrine, writes:

It is as true today as it was then that the doctrine of the Trinity is a theological doctrine derived from the special self-revelation of God, a doctrine which, so far as we can see, could not have been discovered by reason apart from that revelation.[1]

This statement follows a short discussion of the Bible, in which "a post-critical approach" to Holy Scripture is taken for granted and its significance is held to be that of witness to a certain sequence of events or Divine acts in which revelation has been given.

The fixing on events or deeds as the *locus* of Divine revelation, in contrast to words or propositions, was made

[1] *Op. cit.*, p. 25.

an object of special emphasis and elaborate exposition by
the late Archbishop of Canterbury, Dr. Temple, in his
magnum opus, *Nature, Man and God*, and other writings.
Whether it was original with him, or, if not, what its lineage
is, I do not know. In any case it has won wide acceptance
and has become very popular as a theory of revelation.

My purpose is not to criticize the "act" view of revelation
in itself. So far as it goes, it is sound and illuminating. It
may be called the first phase or moment of Divine revelation
as a total process. Dr. Temple makes a great deal also of the
manward or subjective side of revelation. Revelation is to
minds illuminated and inspired to see the activity of God.[1]
This, it seems to me, is the last moment or phase of revelation considered in its wholeness. It is another way of stating
the necessity of what the Protestant Reformers called
testimonium spiritus sancti internum (the internal testimony of
the Holy Ghost). But suspended in the air, so far as this
analysis is concerned, is the problem of the inspiration and
the authoritative significance of the witness of the Bible.
The crux of this problem is in the New Testament and is
brought to a focus when we realize that the New Testament
is only in part a record of events. It is also a record of reflection upon and interpretation of events. It is a book of
doctrine, a series of writings that are theological through
and through. The theology is not always highly developed,
and it is usually not what we should call self-conscious
reflection. It is, in a suggestive phrase of the late Professor
William Sanday of Oxford, referring to the New Testament, "theology in solution."

But it is theology none the less, and ideas are involved
and with them propositions. The propositions that are
primarily interpretative require a judgment as to their
validity and truth, and therefore as to their revelatory significance. To be specific, take John i. 14: "And the Word
became flesh, and dwelt among us (and we beheld His glory,
glory as of the only-begotten of the Father), full of grace
and truth." This is a statement of a doctrine—the doctrine
of the Incarnation. Is it as a proposition simply one man's
private judgment? Or do we have to do with a revelation

---

[1] See *Nature, Man and God*, pp. 312-315; *The Centrality of Christ*, pp. 23-28, 33;
Revelation (ed. Baillie and Martin), pp. 100-107.

of Divine truth, with an interpretation of the meaning of
Jesus Christ inspired by the Holy Spirit and authoritative
for all time?

The same questions might be asked of many other
salient statements and passages of the Bible, as, for example,
"I will pray the Father, and He shall give you another
Comforter,"[1] or "God is love,"[2] or "God is a Spirit,"[3] or
"Upon this rock will I build My Church; and the gates of
Hades shall not prevail against it."[4] And so one might go
on indefinitely. With respect to all the chief attributes of
God, including the mysterious, yet fascinating and infinitely
appealing idea of the Divine holiness, it is not easy to see
how the formula of revelation given simply in act or event
covers the ground.

I believe, accordingly, that there is no alternative to
positing, in the full light of modern criticism, a special inspiration of Holy Scripture. Between the deeds of God and
the acceptance of the revelation given as true by enlightened
minds there is an intermediate moment or phase of revelation. It is the written moment—the moment of recording
and at the same time interpreting.

Revelation, therefore, has three distinct aspects; it covers
in its totality three discrete yet interrelated moments. It
involves (a) specific revelatory acts of God in history;
(b) a definite though not mechanical or magical calling and
inspiring of the Biblical writers to record and interpret the
Divine activity in the events of history; and (c) an illumina-
tion of our minds and hearts so that the revelation testified
to and broadly interpreted in Scripture lays hold on us and
compels our Yea of faith. This may be illustrated in diagrammatic form as follows:

REVELATION

As Perceived by Man.		As Given by God.
A. Event	←————→	Activity.
B. Record	←————→	Inspiration.
C. Apprehension	←————→	Illumination.

This means that as thoughtful Christians we set out from

[1] John xiv. 16.   [2] 1 John iv. 8, 16.
[3] John iv. 24.   [4] Matthew xvi. 18.

the Bible and are under the necessity of labouring to understand it just as much as Athanasius and Chrysostom and
Augustine. We have no other place from which to start
and no other primary source materials on which to work.
Further, the Catholic doctrine has always been that the
Church was founded upon the Scriptures, and not, as is so
frequently heard today, that the Church after all has produced the Bible. This doctrine is also that of the formularies
of the Church of England as well as of the Protestant
Episcopal Church, and it is a doctrine certainly that is as
Evangelical as it is Catholic.

.This does not mean that we can go back to the sixteenth
century or the fourth. It does not mean any refusal of new
light shed by new knowledge. Of both much has been given
the Church of God by modern critical scholarship and, we
are bound to believe, under the guidance of the Spirit of
Truth. We cannot but have a more vivid realization than
past generations (including even a Luther and an Origen)
of the fact that the Bible is human and fallible as well as
Divine and authoritative. The working out of the dialectical
problem set us by this dual character of the Holy Scriptures is not easy. It is not easy for the common man. It is
probably still harder for theologians and scholars. But it is
a task that has to be accepted and worked at with energy
inspired by faith in the continuing presence and guidance
of the Spirit of Truth.

The second step in the basic and initial logic of Trinitarianism concerns the Holy Spirit. To the Father-God of
the Old Testament and the faith of Israel, Christians added,
first, the faith that the man Christ Jesus was the Son of God
and that in being related to Him they were in relation to
very God. They might conceivably have stopped at this
point. If they had done so, we might never have heard of
them, since it was not only as a loose group of believers
in the Messiahship and Resurrection of Christ, but as a
body compacted and knit together in unity by one Spirit
and charged with superhuman energy, that the Church
entered its career as one of the great dominating forces of
history. Still from a theoretical standpoint a Binitarian instead of a Trinitarian view of God was possible; and in
some ways the intellectual task of Christian theologians

would have been lightened had the consciousness of the Church rested in faith in the Father and the Son.

The question, however, is not one of *theory* (as we commonly use the word, denoting by its abstract or *a priori* possibility, and abandoning incidentally its liberal and sounder meaning of "looking at" or "viewing," and hence a generalization from experience), but of *fact*. There is need of reiterated and insistent emphasis on the point that the doctrine of the Trinity did not come into existence as a flight of metaphysical fancy or as the result of a disposition to revel in interesting but inconsequential paradox. It came into existence as an integral *accompaniment* of certain unexpected events that shook, first, the souls of a few elect men, and then the world itself, to the foundations. I use the word "accompaniment" rather than "implication," for it seems to me that the essential doctrine of the Trinity— the view that the object of Christian faith and worship is Three (the Father, the Son, and the Holy Spirit), as well as in some ultimate sense One—was given with the events in which God was seen as speaking and acting for the salvation of the world and for the fulfilment of His purpose in creation. At least it was, as a reflective rational implication, very much fused with apprehension, faith, and the sense of being acted upon in the crucible of total experience.

The second new fact, then, on which Christianity was based and by which its consciousness as a religion was oriented was an extraordinary outpouring of the Spirit of the Lord—the Holy Spirit. The simplest way of getting some idea as to what happened is to keep in mind the psychology of prophecy and prophetism in the Old Testament. The key-feature of the prophetic psychology from the earliest crude beginnings of the prophetic movement through the great major prophets and their Epigoni in the post-exilic Jewish Church is invasion or possession by a power thought to come from beyond the human self. This power was from a comparatively early time in Israel's history identified with the Spirit of Jehovah. The word "spirit" or "breath" bears on it the impress of the desert background and the elemental racial experience of the Hebrew people. It carries with it in all its theological use a reminiscence of "the effortless, empty, eddyless wind of the desert, throbbing past." It signifies the reality of a Divine will, the fact that with God there is energy, activity, and power.

To sum up shortly a long but essentially simple story, the mighty Lord of Hosts (compare the experience of war and battle) was a being who lived and breathed and whose breath was as the wind of the desert, elusive and mysterious, but ever present and not to be resisted. As we speak and express our meaning by means of our wind and breath, so it was on a superhuman and (eventually) an infinite scale with God. When He had something to say, a word to speak, this word was propelled literally on the wings of the wind and, entering into the mouths of chosen prophets as the Divine breath entered their lungs, was uttered by them to their fellows in the name of Jehovah. This explains the close relation between Word and Spirit in the Old Testament, and also the comparative predominance of the latter concept. For speech was but one of the many forms of Divine action. In the Greek tradition, on the other hand, Logos is mainly rational word or idea, and the essence of Divinity is held to lie in the persuasion of reason, not the arbitrary motion of power.

The New Testament is as much or more a record of the activity of the Spirit as the Old Testament. It discloses Christianity as being in its primitive period a "pneumatic" movement. Indeed, the consciousness of the coming of the Holy Spirit and His presence in the Church is so keen that the early Christians regarded themselves as partakers and witnesses of the fulfilment of the prophecy of Joel:

And it shall come to pass afterward, that I will pour out my Spirit upon all flesh; and your sons and your daughters shall prophesy, your old men shall dream dreams, your young men shall see visions: and also upon the servants and upon the handmaids in those days will I pour out my Spirit.[1]

This strain of prophecy, the crown of Old Testament spiritism, is not less important for the early Church than the complex body of Messianic expectation and prediction. The conviction of its fulfilment came no less directly out of experience.

One phase of the revival in the Apostolic Church of a

[1] Joel ii. 28-29.

sense of the Holy Spirit as immediate in presence and power was the return of the ecstatic prophetism. Prophets were as characteristic of the early Church as they were of Israelitish religion in the days of Elijah, and the psychology of prophecy was much the same in both periods, despite a great change in the content of teaching and the direction of interest. Only Apostles outranked Prophets as an order of ministry during the first seventy-five to a hundred years of Church history. Closely related to Christian prophecy from a psychological standpoint was the phenomenon of tongues, together with various special gifts such as "healings," "workings of miracles," and "discernings of spirits." All are referred by St. Paul, along with less spectacular gifts such as teaching, "helps," and "governments," to the working of "that one and the self-same Spirit."[1]

A second aspect of the operation of the Spirit as experienced by the early Christians was a remarkable sense of fellowship and unity. The New Testament word for this is κοινωνία, which means being united or bound together as in a partnership or common enterprise. Christian fellowship or communion was, however, so strongly felt that it was viewed as the special result of the indwelling of the Church by the one Divine Spirit. This is brought out in St. Paul's Trinitarian benediction at the end of the Second Epistle to the Corinthians: "The grace of the Lord Jesus Christ, and the love of God, and the fellowship (κοινωνία) of the Holy Ghost, be with you all."

Finally, the Spirit led and lifted men to new ethical and spiritual levels. His impact was not spent in the extraordinary operations that took human beings outside themselves and their normal consciousness. St. Paul lists as the fruit of the Spirit, over against a very forthright catalogue of the works of the flesh, the following choice virtues: love, joy, peace, longsuffering, kindness, goodness, faithfulness, meekness, self-control.[2] In First Corinthians, without discouraging desire for notable spiritual gifts, and in particular that of prophecy,[3] the Apostle puts *agape* or love as a human attribute above everything else. It is greater

---

[1] I Corinthians xii. [2] Galatians v. 22.
[3] *Cf.* xiv. 3: "He that prophesieth speaketh unto men edification, and exhortation, and consolation."

even than faith or hope.[1] This doctrine is continued and given a kind of theological formulation by St. John in his First Epistle: "For love is of God; and every one that loveth is born of God, and knoweth God."[2]

In the Pauline and Johannine teaching with respect to love in human things we feel that we have to do with something final, with an ultimate boundary, just as truly as we know that we are in the presence of the Absolute when we behold the sacrifice of the Son of God upon His cross. There is a striking parallelism in the two aspects or phases of *agape* in the New Testament. And the parallel holds all the way, for Christlike love as a quality of human life is no more a natural possibility than the life and death of Jesus Christ. We have to do in each case with something Divine— with a transcendent holy love, a *caritas tremenda*, a will of grace that is beyond our human ways and thoughts. In the case of the love of Christ, the explanation is His ultimate nature as the only begotten, Divine Son of God. In the case of the love "shed abroad in our hearts" and the will to abide in that love as children of our Father in heaven, the explanation is in the presence and operation in us of the Holy Spirit and the fact that He, too, is God and is Love.

If we ask, as innumerable modern scholars and writers have done, whether it is necessary to think of the Spirit as personal in the same way as the Son and the Father, the answer is twofold. First, no human being can answer with complete certainty such a query. The doctrine of the Trinity is not something worked out by human ingenuity. It is not the fruit of deliberations by a committee. We are not in a position to prescribe the conditions of Divine existence or the limitations and possibilities of Divine activity. What is certain is that the impact of the Spirit on human life and consciousness was such as to produce the conviction that He was distinct from the Father and the Son and that He was to be co-ordinated with them in worship, in faith, in thought about prayer, and in Baptism or the outward, visible and effectual sign of a new spiritual birth and of membership in the Body of Christ, the Church. Further, the main movement of New Testament thinking about the Spirit is in the direction of ascribing to Him as a Divine

[1] xiii. 13.   [2] iv. 7.

agent personal subjectivity and a distinct relatedness alike to the other Divine persons and to Christian believers.[1]

Second, the clear differentiation of the function or type of activity associated with the Spirit renders appropriate and reasonable the idea of His personal distinctness. The Son exists to reveal. He is the eternal Word of the Father. He is made flesh in order that we may see Him and be drawn toward and have formed in us in idea and motion of the imagination the perfect image of the Father. "I have been crucified with Christ; and it is no longer I that live, but Christ liveth in me."[2] "The riches of the glory of this mystery among the Gentiles, which is Christ in you, the hope of glory."[3] "But we all, with unveiled face beholding as in a mirror the glory of the Lord, are transformed into the same image from glory to glory, even as from the Lord the Spirit."[4] Even so—even as dwelling in a sense within us and in the way of supplanting our old self as contributor of the master-principle of our lives—our Lord remains a distinct object. Our relation to Him religiously is as our Saviour, Physician, Friend, Elder Brother and Great High Priest. It is a relation of communion as between two persons. In this relation we are aware of the attraction and the drawing power of an influence, but our sense of freedom and of responsible self-determination remains clear and at its maximum.

The Spirit, on the other hand, acts, and exists to act, in a very different manner. He is the agent of the Divine will. He is in His very nature a compelling energy, an activating force. His it is to enter into the recesses of the human spirit and to work from within the subjectivity of man. This operation is invisible and only partly an object of consciousness and knowledge to us. "The wind bloweth where it listeth, and thou hearest the sound thereof, but canst not tell from whence it cometh, and whither it goeth; so is every one that is born of the Spirit."[5] From within our human being the Spirit vitalizes, stabilizes, renews, admonishes, warns, recalls, interprets, enlightens, guides and

---

[1] In addition to Matthew xxviii. 19 and 2 Corinthians xiii. 14, the reader is referred especially to 1 Corinthians ii. 10-12; Romans viii. 16-19, 26-27; Ephesians ii. 18, iv. 4-5, 30; John xiv. 16-17, 25-26; xv. 26-27; xvi. 7-14.

[2] Galatians ii. 20.   [3] Colossians i. 27.

[4] 2 Corinthians iii. 18.   [5] John iii. 8.

gives comfort (or strength). He is God in His special
activity and agency of secret invasion and invisible occupation. His Divine task is to bore from within, not in the
service of an infernal Gestapo, but in unrelenting warfare
against the invisible powers of evil and as the Minister of
the prevenient goodness and lovingkindness of the Lord.

This relation of the Holy Spirit to man, both as redeemed
(that is, as in Christ through faith and Baptism and responsive and responsible Church membership) and as not yet
redeemed, is best described as invasion or possession. The
second term has been given wide currency in this context,
in distinction from the religious relation of communion,
as a result of an essay by the present Bishop of Oxford, Dr.
Kirk, published nearly two decades ago in the volume
Essays on the Trinity and the Incarnation. It should be borne in
mind that the possession by the Spirit of God, like its opposite, possession by evil powers or spirits, whatever be our
ultimate metaphysical interpretation of this ancient and
New Testament mode of thought, is not necessarily absolute or static and unvarying. It is generally a matter of
degree and is one element in an interplay of forces constituting our psychic life, in which also freedom and moral
responsibility are another factor.

Let us take a simple but crucial illustration—namely, our
growth as Christians in the greatest of Christian virtues:
agape, or charity or love. The Book of Common Prayer
teaches with the utmost force and clarity that without this
quality "all our doings . . . are nothing worth" and "who-
soever liveth is counted dead before Thee" (Collect for
Quinquagesima, or the Sunday next before Lent). So far as
we are growing up toward the love of Christ, and are
having this love built into our inmost nature and character
as a master-motive, we know that this is happening in spite
of ourselves fully as much as because of ourselves. It is
happening because the grace of God is not only something
without us, manifest in the death and passion of Jesus
Christ, but is a power at work within us, directing its
impact at the very citadel of our wills. This inward grace is
God personally at work within us. It is God the Holy
Ghost.

Since writing the paragraph immediately preceding this

I have come across some sentences from St. Augustine which express so exactly the point I have tried to make that I set them down as a conclusion to this exposition of the place of the Spirit in Christian religion.

It is by love that we are conformed to God, and this is due to the Holy Spirit. But in no way could we be restored by the Holy Spirit, unless He Himself remained unimpaired and unchangeable; and this could not be unless He were of the Divine nature and substance.

There is no gift of God that can surpass this (*i.e.*, love). It alone distinguishes the sons of the eternal kingdom and the sons of eternal perdition. . . . Love, therefore, which is of God and is God, is specially the Holy Spirit, by whom the love of God is shed abroad in our hearts, by which love the whole Trinity dwells in us.[1]

If we are thus related, in a manner at once essential and distinctive, to the Holy Spirit, and if this relation in no way replaces but rather requires relatedness to Jesus Christ as Revealer of God, Lord, and Saviour, and to our Creator and Heavenly Father, the transcendent Lord of all Being, the final resting-place of all thought and all worship and all hope, then it is reasonable to suppose that the Spirit is a distinct person of the Trinity, not the Father and not the Son, though one with them in a perfect unity of life, being, mind, will and consciousness. Such is the basis of the Trinity as a Christian doctrine. It is perhaps not so much a basis as a root out of which stems organically and by an inwardly controlled necessity a plant or vine or tree. This root is itself trinal or threefold in form. It is the Trinitarian nature of Christianity as a religion.

[1] *On the Morals of the Catholic Church*, 13 (23); *On the Trinity*, xv. 32.

There was at first nothing whatever that is begotten; the Father was in solitude, unbegotten. . . . But inasmuch as He had the faculty of generation, it seemed good to Him at last to bring to birth and to put forth what He had within Himself that was fairest and most perfect; for He was no lover of solitude. For He was, the writer says, all Love; but love is not love, unless there be an object of love.

VALENTINUS (c. A.D. 150).

Always God, always Son, at the same time Father, at the same time Son, the Son exists unbegotten with the Father, everlasting, uncreated, neither in conception nor in any smallest point does God excel the Son.

ALEXANDER, BISHOP OF ALEXANDRIA (†A.D. 326).

The Holy Spirit . . . is something common both to the Father and the Son. But that communion itself is consubstantial and co-eternal; and if it may fitly be called friendship, let it be so called; but it is more aptly called love. . . . But love is of some one that loves, and with love something is loved.

ST. AUGUSTINE (A.D. 354-430).

The Living and True God was from all Eternity, and from all Eternity wanted like a God.

THOMAS TRAHERNE (A.D. 1636?-1674).

Hail, holy Light, offspring of Heaven first-born!
Or of the Eternal co-eternal beam
May I express thee unblamed? since God is light,
And never but in unapproachèd light
Dwelt from eternity—dwelt then in thee,
Bright effluence of bright essence increate!

JOHN MILTON (A.D. 1608-1674).

74

CHAPTER IV

What is the Doctrine of the Trinity?

THE Christian religion is, in the first instance, a story or epic. It is the narrative of the acts and words of God to men, performed and uttered with a view to disclosing His Divine nature and will and to rescuing and putting back on the right track the special object of His love—the race of men. The Bible is the record of God's self-revelation as Creator, Ruler of the nations, Giver of law, Tutor and Disciplinarian of humanity; as Redeemer, Lover of men, Provider of sacrifice for sin, Seeker of reconciliation, Forgiver of transgressions, Physician of souls; and as Sanctifier, Convicter of the world "in respect of sin, and of righteousness, and of judgment,"[1] Inspirer of holiness, truth and beauty, Giver, Preserver and Increaser of Spiritual life.

The Bible was written by inspired men, who yet remained men and therefore weak and fallible. It is not sheer miracle; it is not comparable to transcription from a Divinely arranged and loaded dictaphone. It is in a real sense a single, unified work; yet it is in two main divisions that are discontinuous as well as continuous. Each division or Testament, furthermore, is made up of numerous individual compositions or compilations, written at different times and containing the impress of varied interests and points of view. In the case of the Old Testament we have to do with a literary work that resembles nothing so much as an infinitely complex geological formation. The layers or strata are all there, but there has been such a criss-crossing of faults at points that it is next to impossible to unscramble and rearrange them in chronological order. Then the parts, although all have a definite contribution to make, are not of equal value. Discrimination and sound judgment in "dividing the Word of truth"[2] are not an option but a necessity. Even the Canon is a problem as well as a fact. The omission of certain Apocryphal books is from the Christian standpoint, as many of the ablest Christian Fathers saw, unjustifiable and a serious loss.

[1] John xvi. 8. [2] 2 Timothy ii. 15.

All this means that in the Bible we have to do with a human process, which may be and should be approached and studied from a scientific point of view. It means, further, that pure Biblicism is unsound. The Scriptures need as an auxiliary of understanding and interpretation the tradition of the Church. Here the *Articles of Religion*, weaving their way deftly if cumbersomely between the Scylla of extreme Protestantism and the Charibdis of unmitigated Catholicism, are fundamentally sound. Article XX could hardly be improved on. Article VIII could bring out more clearly than it does the fact that the Creeds, by the grace of the Holy Ghost, have a contribution of their own to bring to the right use and understanding of Holy Scripture.

Yet the Bible remains, when all is said and done, the greatest miracle of all time. It is in actuality the Word of God, since it is only through its witness, record and interpretation that we confront and are confronted by the deeds and the speech of the living God. In it is set down once and for all the epic story which is the Gospel of God, the Father, the Son, and the Holy Spirit.

Christianity, in the second place, is doctrine. It is a body of doctrines.[1] A doctrine, as we saw in Chapter II, is a view of reality in some aspect. It is a formulation of a more or less general truth required by a certain body of facts. It is an inference from cogent and definitely implicative evidence. A Christian doctrine is a statement of some truth, either given with the Gospel or implied by the Gospel, taken in connection with all possible relevant facts. Among the Christian doctrines are the Creation, the Incarnation, the Atonement, the Holy Spirit, and the Trinity. These, together with Church and Sacraments, which are closely related to the Holy Spirit; Grace, which includes or rather intersects them all; and Eternal Life, the great Consequent emerging ineradicably from all, constitute the primary Christian doctrines.

---

[1] The word "dogmas" could be used equally well, if with less precision. The number of Christian dogmas, if we stick to a rigid definition and use the term to mean an enacted and authoritatively set forth view or teaching, is small. The General Councils were pretty well occupied with two subjects, the Trinity and the Incarnation. Yet who would question that there is a Christian dogma, or doctrine carrying weight or authority, of the Atonement, of the Eucharist, of man, etc.?

The doctrine of the Trinity is the most comprehensive and the most nearly all-inclusive formulation of the truth of Christianity. It is in and of itself a not inadequate summation of the principal teachings of the Christian religion. This doctrine is the view that the Father, the Son, and the Holy Spirit of Scripture and the Creeds and the universal continuing consciousness of the Christian Church, ever to be worshipped and glorified as distinct, individual, personal determinations and centres of Godhead, are nevertheless one God—one single, unified Divine essence or being. In phraseology suggested in part by the ancient Catechism of the Church of England, the doctrine of the Trinity is the teaching that God, who as the Father hath made me and all the world, who as the Son hath redeemed me and all mankind, and who as the Holy Ghost sanctifieth me and all the people of God, is within the unity and perfection of His eternal being Three as well as One, and that the Divine Three are mutually and personally related to one another.

There are various other ways of stating the doctrine or dogma of the Trinity. One of the simplest of all classical statements, which yet seems to be a rock of stumbling to most people, perhaps because of its calculated severity of paradox and economy of speculative admixture, is the declaration of the so-called Athanasian Creed:[1]

So the Father is God, the Son is God: and the Holy Ghost is God. And yet they are not three gods: but one God. So likewise the Father is Lord, the Son Lord: and the Holy Ghost Lord. And yet not three Lords: but one Lord. For like as we are compelled by the Christian verity: to acknowledge every person by himself to be God and Lord; So are we forbidden by the Catholick religion; to say, There be three Gods, or three Lords.

This formulation of the Trinity is really a bald transcript of the salient ideas of the Nicene Creed (of which it may have originally been an exposition or commentary, hence the name "Athanasian") under the influence of the Trinitarian theology of St. Augustine. It accents the mystery of the Divine Trinity, the necessity of accepting it on authority, and at the same time the absolute equality of the three Persons.

[1] Included in all English Books of Common Prayer beginning with 1549 and including the "Deposited" Book of 1928; omitted in all American Books beginning with the first "proposed" Book, which was never approved by a General Convention.

Another fine statement, minimal in content of thought yet careful in hewing to the line of perfect orthodoxy, and flawless in distinction of style, is that of Article I, the title of which, very significantly, is simply: "Of Faith in the Holy Trinity." It reads:

There is but one living and true God, everlasting, without body, parts, or passions; of infinite power, wisdom, and goodness; the Maker and Preserver of all things both visible and invisible. And in unity of this Godhead there be three Persons, of one substance, power, and eternity; the Father, the Son, and the Holy Ghost.

This formulary incorporates the technical Trinitarian terms long established in the usage of the Latin West—namely, "substance" from *substantia* (=concrete being, including both the sum of attributes and the unique principle of individuality) and "person" from *persona* (=a permanent, individual mode or manner of Divine existence). It is a useful introduction to the greatest and weightiest short statement of the doctrine of the Trinity on record—that of the Eastern Bishops and Doctors assembled in Constantinople in A.D. 382 (the year after what we now know as the Second General Council). This statement occurs as part of a Synodal Letter addressed to Damasus, Ambrosius, and the rest of the Bishops "assembled in the great city of Rome." After speaking of the many sufferings undergone "for the sake of the Evangelical faith, ratified by three hundred and eighteen fathers at Nicea in Bithynia," "the orthodox bishops" proceed:

This is the faith which ought to be sufficient for you, for us, for all who wrest not the word of the true faith; for it is the ancient faith; it is the faith of our Baptism; it is the faith that teaches us to believe in the name of the Father, of the Son, and of the Holy Ghost. According to this faith there is one Godhead, Power and Being (οὐσία) of the Father and of the Son and of the Holy Ghost; the dignity being equal, and the majesty being equal in three perfect hypostases—*i.e.*, three perfect persons.

Several things in this formulation of the doctrine of the Trinity are noteworthy. First, there is the emphasis upon the Evangelical (referring of course to the Gospel) character of the Nicene Creed and a kindred stress upon the relation between Baptism and the faith of the Trinity. (Let the reader recall here what we said about the Matthean Baptismal Formula in the last chapter). Second, it is a dogmatic, not a speculative or philosophical statement. No attempt is made to explain or clarify or illuminate the conception of a God who is both One and Three. Third, technical terms are used: the Greek word for "being," of which "substance" (see above) is a common translation; "hypostasis," a transliteration of a Greek word meaning "that which stands under," and hence that which supports in being various attributes or a concrete individual determination of being; and the Greek word for person, this being equated with hypostasis and recalled to Trinitarian use for the first time since Sabellius. Fourth, a perfect equality of the Three persons is asserted. Here, as in the revival of the word "person," East and West may be seen as drawing together after a long period of sharp divergence in thought as well as confusion of language. We have, in fact, in the declaration of the Synod of Constantinople a clear indication that the Church in respect of its Trinitarian consciousness has come of age. Henceforth there is general agreement that the God of Christian faith is "one Being in three Hypostases," or "one Substance in three Persons."

Or, finally, apart from technical terms, we may perhaps say that the Christian doctrine of the Trinity is the doctrine that the one, living, and true God, who has manifested Himself as Father, as Son, and as the Holy Spirit, is within Himself also, in a real and concrete manner, three. He is a Trinity of persons within a fundamental and absolute unity of being, consciousness, and will.

Christian worship affords numerous specific illustrations. Worship is directed to God as Trinity and as Unity. Sometimes the accent falls on one aspect, sometimes on the other. With us who are creatures, and who are reaching out in trust and adoration to that which is infinitely great and therefore beyond the best efforts of our thought and imagination to understand and picture, such an alteration of emphasis is as proper as it is inevitable. What is important intellectually is that a balance be maintained.

Take, for example, Reginald Heber's Trinitarian hymn, to the writer the premier hymn in the English language. The first and last stanzas stress in the context of the strikingly symbolic *Trisagion*—"Holy, Holy, Holy"—the Divine

Trinity. The first stanza ends, and the hymn ends, with the line:

"God in three persons, blessed Trinity."

This is the overshadowing impression conveyed by the hymn: that God in His eternal praiseworthiness, in His impenetrable yet not unillumined mysteriousness and in His unconcealed glory, is a Trinity. Yet if the hymn be studied carefully one will see that it is "the Lord God Almighty," "perfect in power, in love, and purity," of whom the singular personal pronouns "Thee," "Thou" and "Thy" are used consistently, who is the "blessed Trinity."

A second, very obvious illustration is the *Gloria Patri* ("Glory be to the Father, and to the Son, and to the Holy Ghost; as it was in the beginning, is now, and ever shall be, world without end"). This *Gloria* is probably used more often in Episcopalian (or Anglican) worship than it is in the regular services of any other Christian Church. (Monastic offices may be an exception.) It contains no direct reference, even by implication, to the unity of God. In this it is like the New Testament, where the foreground is dominated by God's revelation of Himself in word and act and distributive personal manifestation as Father, as Son, and as Holy Spirit. The monotheism of Israel is there; there is no thought of denying it or calling it into question; but it remains in the background. The primary object of concern in each case is God the Father, God the Son, and God the Holy Spirit.

For everyday use in Christian worship this is sufficient. Yet it is good to have an occasional variation even in the Liturgy, which drives home the point that the great central theologians in the ancient Catholic Church (Irenæus, Tertullian, Athanasius and Augustine) found themselves obliged to defend with might and main—namely, that Christians believe in and worship one God. Such a variation is found in the amplified conclusion of a number of classical collects: "through Jesus Christ our Lord, who liveth and reigneth with Thee and the Holy Ghost, one God, world without end." Even more striking and more nearly perfect as an expression of the paradox of the Christian doctrine of God is the special doxology found in the present American Book of Common Prayer as the close of the *Benedicite*, commonly sung since 1549 in Lent instead of the *Te Deum*. It reads:

> Let us bless the Father, and the Son, and the Holy Ghost: praise *him*, and magnify *him* for ever.[1]

Other illustrations, among almost any number that could be cited, are the fourth invocation of the opening section of the English Litany as composed by Archbishop Cranmer just over four hundred years ago, and the Collect for Trinity Sunday. In the Litany as Cranmer composed it one prays, after invoking severally and individually the three persons of the Trinity:

> O holy, blessed, and glorious Trinity, three Persons and one God: have mercy upon us miserable sinners.

In the American Book of Common Prayer as revised in 1928 in line with the old Sarum Litany this invocation was cut down drastically and was divided between Minister and people instead of being repeated in full. It now reads:

> O holy, blessed, and glorious Trinity, one God: *Have mercy upon us.*

In this form the accent is more on the oneness of God. The Trinity Collect, as contained without alteration in all "Anglican" Prayer Books, states in perfect balance the Christian doctrine of Trinity in Unity:

> Almighty and everlasting God, who hast given unto thy servants grace, by the confession of a true faith, to acknowledge the glory of the eternal Trinity, and in the power of the Divine Majesty to worship the Unity; we beseech thee that thou wouldest keep us stedfast in this faith, and evermore defend us from all adversities; who livest and reignest, one God, world without end.

This prayer is equally useful both as a plain man's guide and as a theologian's compass needle in thinking about and in blessing and adoring that Divine Trinity which is the one only and eternal God, the Lord of all being and the Maker and Preserver of all things, visible and invisible.

Such is the doctrine or dogma of the Trinity. Such is the Christian religion as doctrine in at least its major and most inclusive single formulation. If what we said in Chapter III

---

[1] Italics mine. This doxology was introduced into the Revised American Prayer Book of 1928. It is evidently taken from the Roman Breviary, where it forms a part of the special doxology that follows the *Benedicite* in the service of *Lauds*. This doxology is said to have been composed by Pope Damasus (†A.D. 384).

about the Trinitarian character of Christianity as a religion is remembered, and if we keep in mind the vital connection between this religion as epic or Gospel and as doctrine, we shall feel and respect the significance of such unelaborated and unadorned statements of the doctrine of the Trinity as those just noted and presented. They are utterly necessary as a preliminary intellectual and moral and liturgical or devotional step. They are required by the Christian facts, and they illuminate in turn, and vivify and throw into clear focus, alike for the faithful and for the inquiring, the mighty acts and the adorable being of the blessed God.

Yet this type of formulation, indispensable as it is, is not a final goal. It represents, at best, a half-way house for the mind and also for the heart—for the affections and the will. By and for itself it is bound to prove unsatisfactory. This is the reaction of ordinary people to the doctrine of the Trinity, baldly stated, and to other doctrines as well. Theologians have nearly always shared this reaction and have tried to carry further the work of Christian thought. They have tried to think through, so far as possible, the implications of the various doctrines of the Christian faith and then to relate them to the world viewed as a whole, taking into account the knowledge made available at any given period by science, psychology and philosophy. This gives us the key to Christianity in its third phase or stage. *Christianity is, thirdly, a philosophy.* It is a world view. It is a systematic map of the real, drawn up in the light of the self-revelation of God in Jesus Christ.

Evidently, in such a structure the key-stone of the main arch is the doctrine of God. This statement applies to every positive philosophy if, instead of the word "God," we read "Ultimate" or "Supreme Real." It applies to materialism, Platonism, Stoicism, Spinozism, idealism, positivism, Marxism, and National Socialism, as much as to Christianity.

The God of Christianity is a Trinitarian God. The Christian Ultimate is a super-personal union of three Divine Persons—the Father, the Son, and the Holy Spirit. Yet this union is not something impersonal. It is not an abstract common nature such as our minds discern when they compare the members of a species, as, for example, tigers or men. The universal (the technical name for tigerhood or manhood or justice or liberty) is in some sense real, as Aristotle saw, over and above its existence *post rem* (after the thing) in the perceiving and analyzing mind. But this reality, whatever it is—whether simply in individuals (*in re*) or as an idea first in the mind of God (*ante rem*)—is an impersonal abstraction.

Or, again, the union of the Divine Three is more than the unity of spirit that may exist between two people bound together closely in love or friendship. This mystical unity is likewise real; it may seem to be a new creation, and incapable of ever ceasing to be. Perhaps in God there is a possibility of perpetuity for high human relationships. Yet the most exalted human unities do not achieve, so far as we know, a hypostatic (from hypostasis—see above) or personal condition. And experience teaches us that they partake deeply, also, of man's transitoriness and variability. They may, and not infrequently do, pass into a virtual nothingness.

Then there is the union of members of a group—a family, a clan, a school, a race, or a nation. These names denote real entities. Such entities seem to be capable of generating a certain group spirit, which may be an extremely powerful thing, able to absorb into itself for the time being the individual spirits that make up the group. We are today vividly aware of this possibility and of the threat inherent in it to the individual, scientific, and even religious integrity. But its metaphysics, if not its psychology, remains obscure. It is a testimony to the social and finite character of a man and to the fact of his creation for community. There is, however, no evidence that the spirit of a group is real in the persistent, concrete sense in which a horse is real or a man is real. We do outgrow in America some stages at least of "school spirit," and in Great Britain some transcendence of the "school tie" is not unknown even in conservative circles. When a Napoleon or a Hitler is overthrown, and with him both the myth of invincibility and the power of the communal spirit engendered by his personal magnetism and mastery of the word, individual followers remain to experience disillusionment and often to react in hate.

There is in fact no human analogy that is more than weakly partial or faintly suggestive when we come to the Unity of the Trinitarian God. The Christian doctrine is not one of three Gods or Lords, however sublimated the polytheism proposed, however closely united in concord, fraternity, affinity, and a common purpose the Divine Three are held to be. It is the doctrine of one God—one ultimate Divine being, life, mind, will, and consciousness. This God is Himself a "Thou" or a "He." The Trinity as a whole is to be identified with the Jehovah of the Old Testament, as St. Augustine clearly saw. We can speak of "they" or even "the Three" only relatively in relation to the fact of One God. Here the Athanasian Creed has an importance all its own, which has not been outgrown.

So the question arises and is insistent, How can this be? How can the human mind grasp and make real to its thought or in its imagination this stupendous but baffling conception of the Trinity in Unity and the Unity in Trinity?

From an early time Christian thinkers have faced and wrestled with this problem thus set them. At first the solution did not seem difficult. The analogy widely used, following St. John's Prologue and Philo, was that of the Word —uttering thought or expressing ideas. This is in a sense a psychological approach to the problem. Psychology was, however, much less important to the first Christian theologians, who were as a whole conspicuously Greek-minded, than cosmology (=science of the world) and transcendental theology (a God so perfect metaphysically that He cannot be in direct touch with the world). The Logos or Word had, therefore, a double value: He explained the rationality of the world (its being a cosmos) and He connected the world with the transcendent Father. His being Himself a secondary or subordinate deity—a god "in the second rank"(Justin Martyr) or "intermediate between the nature of the Uncreated and that of created things" (Origen)— fitted in perfectly with the numerous utterances of our Lord and His interpreters in the New Testament that seemed to teach a subordination of the Son. The fallacy in this, as a mature theology pointed out in time, was a failure to distinguish between the pre-existent, eternal Godhead of the Son and His Incarnate condition—His living a human life and having a human will and consciousness. Furthermore, such a Christology (=science of Christ) could never do justice to the heart of New Testament Christianity—namely, that God was verily in Christ and that the Divine love expressing itself in His sacrifice was of the very nature of Absolute Deity.

A second attempt at solving the problem presented by the Trinity was made early in the third century. It was made in Rome by a man named Sabellius. His proposal was startling in its originality and simplicity. He advocated, in a word, untying the Gordian knot by cutting it in two. God is one; He is the Divine monad. This is the clear teaching of the Scriptures. It is equally clear that God appeared to men and made Himself known as Father, as Son, and as Holy Spirit. Both things being true, the obvious solution is that the Trinity is one of manifestation. God is like an actor on the Greek stage; He is able to take different parts at different times by putting on a new mask or face. (This is the literal and original meaning of the Greek word for person, πρόσωπον, which was applied by Sabellius to the rôles of Father, Son and Spirit.) He was influenced, I believe, at this point by noting (a) that in the Old Testament God patently appears in diverse ways, and (b) that according to the Fourth Gospel the Holy Spirit does not come until the Son is glorified.[1]

The Sabellian interpretation of the Trinity is tenable only if we allow such an exposition of "one place of Scripture, that it be repugnant to another" (Article XX). It does irreparable violence to the Christian facts. It is, further, a highly sophisticated and a too cleverly simple view. Yet it had two strong points, which have left a permanent impress upon subsequent Trinitarian theology. It taught that the Persons of the Trinity were entirely equal and that Christ was fully God. Neither point was ever forgotten in Western teaching, and both were ultimately accepted, with only the slightest modification in respect of the first, by Greek or Eastern theology.

It is unnecessary to say anything more about the contribution of St. Athanasius to thought regarding the Trinity. As brought out at length in Chapter III his work was to

[1] John vii. 39. *Cf.* the passages already cited in xiv.-xvi.

assert the Trinitarian character of Christianity as a religion. He put great emphasis, too, upon the unity of God. An Oxford lecturer on theology used to say in his classroom, with pardonable exaggeration, that "Athanasius was the only man in the fourth century who was more afraid of polytheism than of unitarianism." But he elected to stay out of the deeper waters of speculation and analogical research with a view to greater understanding. In this respect he resembles a great Christian and Bishop of the late second century, St. Irenæus of Lyons in Gaul.

The first real theologians of the Trinity, after the Council of Nicea and the long-drawn-out but decisive and final repulse of Arianism, were the so-called Cappadocian Fathers—Basil of Cæsarea, Gregory of Nyssa, and Gregory of Nazianzus. There are the men behind the formula of Constantinople in A.D. 382, cited and emphasized above. They were typical Easterners, university men, trained in logic and philosophy. They were for a time under semi-Arian influence (the most conservative school of Arianism which was willing to say that Christ was of *like* but not *the same* substance as the Father—*homoiousion* not *homoousion*—and thus gave Gibbon and Carlyle the chance to invent neat epigrams on the theme that the fate of the world hung on an iota or i). They used in their earlier thinking the analogy of three men and a common manhood. They were prepared, even as mature theologians, to see the Christian doctrine of the Trinity as a *via media* between Judaism and Paganism. They set out instinctively from the reality of the Trinity, conceived as given with Christianity itself, and then sought to reconcile the threeness of God with His unity.

The solution which the Cappadocians reached was something like this: Each Divine person (hypostasis was their term—see definition above) was entirely and perfectly God. He partook without addition or subtraction of the Divine essence or being. He had every attribute of Godhead. He differed from the other two Persons only in having a distinct subsistence (=absolute existence, such as only God has). The idea of generation (compare the Nicene Creed: "begotten, not made") was carefully separated from its human and finite associations and pared down to mean a permanent, eternally distinct mode of Divine existence (τρόπος ὑπάξεως). No more could be said of the distinct existence of the Father except that He was logically prior to the Son. Of the distinct person of the Spirit, likewise, no further specific definition could be given. This is the basis for the unconsciously dry remark of the Greek Summist or Summarizer of Doctrine, John of Damascus, in the eighth century:

> The Holy Spirit is from the Father, not by generation, but by procession; that there is a difference between the two we have been taught, but wherein they differ we know not.

It would be easy to gain from a bare summary of this kind the impression that the Cappadocian Fathers were dry-as-dust logicians and no more. This would be to do them a grave injustice. There is in their writings, especially perhaps those of Gregory of Nazianzus, a spirit of devotion and a sense of rapt adoration in the very thought of the Blessed Trinity that are not unworthy of comparison with anything in the history of Christian literature. Here is a sample from the Gregory just mentioned:

> Adoring Father, Son, and Holy Ghost; knowing the Father in the Son, and the Son in the Holy Ghost—into whose names we were baptized, in which we have believed; under whose banner we have been enlisted; dividing Them before we combine Them, and combining before we divide; not receiving the Three as one Person (for they are not impersonal or names of one Person, as though our wealth lay in names alone and not in facts), but the three as one Thing for they are One, not in Person but in Godhead, Unity adored in Trinity, and Trinity summed up in Unity; all adorable, all royal, of one throne and one glory; above the world, above time, uncreated, invisible, impalpable, uncircumscript; in Its relation to Itself known only to Itself but to us equally venerable and adorable; alone dwelling in the Holiest, and leaving all creatures outside and shut off.

This passage brings out a special quality of Cappadocian Trinitarianism. No theologians have ever been more convinced than these Fathers of the reality of the Trinity or more resolute in their faith. For them God is first and foremost the Father, the Son, and the Holy Spirit. They reveal no disposition to explain away the Divine Threeness, in an ultimately Sabellian manner, as a necessity of our thought arising out of the division and plurality native to us. At the same time it must be confessed that the Cappadocians tended to solve the problem in terms of logical abstractions and to be satisfied with the result. They evince no interest in psychology or the social nature of man as affording possibly an analogical purchase for vaulting into the empyrean of high speculation. It is here that St. Augustine comes into the picture.

In Augustine's work on the Trinity all previous major influences converge. In some cases they are pruned of excess and always they are reforged in the crucible of his own mind, but they are there. The essentially psychological analogy of the rational Word is present. The Sabellian note of an absolute equality of the three Persons is present. So is the strongly monotheistic and Biblical slant on the Divine unity that was characteristic of Athanasius; and also the "modal" interpretation of the three Persons, with each identically God from the standpoint of being or all concrete qualities. Finally, Augustine introduces into Trinitarian thought an appeal to the Johannine dictum, "God is Love," and in his analysis of it utilizes necessarily the analogy of human love and friendship. This was not a totally new idea. The great Gnostic Valentinus, in the second century, had a not dissimilar idea. (See the quotation at the head of this chapter.) Presumably it was the excess of the Gnostic mythology that brought into disrepute this approach. Also, as has happened several times since, Christianity gave reason a new lease on life. It was rational categories that attracted the Greek Christian Fathers. With the analogy of love Augustine combined the notion of the Spirit as the union or communion of the Father and the Son. This common bond is love, in distinction from lover and object of love. From this combination of conceptions is derived the thought that the Holy Spirit is in a special sense Love.

Such was the inheritance of St. Augustine as he undertook, not wholly willingly, the task of endeavouring to understand more clearly the mystery of the Trinity. In some ways it was an embarrassment of riches. Also Augustine was a true Christian in having a sense of intellectual as well as personal humility. He was keenly aware of the limitations of the human mind. In his long and repetitious work *On the Trinity* he is constantly urging his inability to get far in his chosen task. The mystery of light is too great.

It blinds. (This must be the present writer's defence, too, if in the end the reader feels a sense of disappointment in the answer given to the question which is the title of this chapter.).

Still Augustine did pursue, with energy and persistence, his aim. Briefly, these are the conclusions which he reached. The Scriptures teach that the one God, who is Creator of the world, is a Trinity. They speak not only of a Father who is God, but of an only begotten Son Jesus Christ, who is God made man, and of a Holy Spirit, who is likewise God. The Son, as His name implies, is generated or begotten. This is best understood by examining our own minds and their power of knowledge. The Son of God is eternally generated as the object of the Divine self-knowledge. With God, however, such a relation is subsistent and personal. It is the Divine substance or Godhead in a distinct mode of existence, and is absolutely equal to the Father. There is no subordination.

Augustine then carries his psychological analogy a step further. As there is generated within the mind of God a perfect object, so there proceeds an accompanying motion of His will, which is Love. This love, which is of the Son or Divine *alter ego*, is likewise a personal relation. It is the Godhead in a distinct mode of existence. The third Person, also, is on an absolute equality with the other two, and is equal to the entire Trinity. Both as Spirit (John iv. 24) and as Love (1 John iv. 8, 16) He is in a special manner the content of Deity or, as Augustine liked to say, the *vinculum* or bond uniting the Father and the Son.

Is this Trinity social or not? Is the eternal Divine love to be conceived in line with the analogy of human affection or in terms of self-love? This is a problem on which I have pondered a long time. No certain answer, I presume, can be given. Augustine starts out, after opening up the analysis of the proposition "God is Love," on a social tack. Then he gets cold feet and spends most of his remaining space on analogies derived from individual human personality. But now and again he is drawn back to the first idea. He was, it would seem, powerfully attracted to the idea of a communion of Father and Son within the unity of the Holy Spirit, whose special name is Love. But he was unable to see the compatibility of genuine sociability in God with the Divine unity, which he conceived, in company with all rational philosophers and theologians of antiquity, mathematically and rigidly, not as an organic manifold—at once single and plural.

In any case it was the image of the solitary thinker and solitary lover that became the standard rationale of the Trinity for the next fifteen hundred years. There is, I believe, no evidence (here Dean Rashdall was right) that St. Thomas Aquinas entertained any notion of a Divine sociality. Indeed, he appears to wish it to be understood explicitly that altereity in a social sense is not required by the concept of infinite or perfect goodness.[1] There are sporadic appeals to Augustine's *dicta* on love, and occasionally a writer, like Richard of St. Victor (*c.* A.D. 1150) sets forth boldly a social doctrine of the Trinity. Bishop George Bull in the late seventeenth century, in responding to the request of an English lord for an explanation of the Trinity, put forward a social construction with a eudaimonistic tinge. Since God must be thought of as having "self-sufficiency and most perfect bliss and happiness in Himself alone, before and without all created beings . . . it plainly appears that Himself alone is a most perfect and blessed society, the Father, the Son, and the Spirit eternally conversing with and enjoying one another."

Broadly speaking, however, the psychological analogy of St. Augustine commanded the field until Hegel. (The Reformers eschewed rational speculation as much as possible, but this renunciation included also any social analogy.) The parallel between the influence of the *City of God* of Augustine and that of his *On the Trinity* is very close. As it was Hegel who put forward a new philosophy of history in terms not of two opposing cities corresponding to opposing loves, but of the self-evolution of one Absolute Spirit, so it was he who revived the Philonic and Greek Christian speculation that the generation of the Son was the creation of the world. Following Augustine, however, and at the same time altering him, Hegel made the Spirit the focus of Divine unity, or, in his terminology, the final and absolute moment in the process of the Divine self-consciousness.

---

[1] *Summa Theologica*, "Treatise on the Trinity," Qu. 32, art. 1 (ad secundum).

For Hegel the world ultimately is God and God is the innermost, true reality of the world. (See, further, Chapter II.)

The second major development in nineteenth century Trinitarianism was a very widespread conscious turning to a social doctrine of God. By the end of the century this trend had assumed the proportions of a landslip[1] on a continental scale. Undoubtedly it was in part a reflection in theology of the instinct manifest in social reform, socialism, the Social Gospel so called, social psychology, and the various social sciences. From literally scores of possible illustrations of the new emphasis we select a few sentences from a volume published in 1903 by an eminent American divine, born in Scotland, George A. Gordon. Gordon went to Harvard College after he had finished a theological seminary, and became a serious student of Greek philosophy. It is said that he was accustomed to read the works of Aristotle in the original for his winter reading, and the dialogues of Plato for his summer reading. On one occasion he remarked of these two thinkers, "Everything is in them."

For Gordon the truth behind the symbol of the Trinity is "the essentially social nature of God; the faith that He is in His innermost being an eternal family." "Love in man is passion for another; its existence depends upon the society in which a man is placed. Love in God must mean passion for another; its reality depends upon the society in the Godhead." "The Christian doctrine of the Trinity is the full statement of the truth at which Greek mythology aimed. . . . Put into the Godhead some reality answering to the words, the Father and the Son and the Holy Spirit, and one is able to conceive of God's existence as ineffably blessed, and as containing in itself the ground of human society."

Such a view, at first largely accepted, ran in time into heavy opposition. In one of his first published works, *The Nature of Personality*, the late Archbishop William Temple (then a young philosophy don at Oxford) wrote: "We are not . . . called upon to handle riddles such as, How can God be Love if there is no object for His love? For there is the whole Universe for such object." Professor Pringle-

---

[1] Or landslide.

Pattison directed to this version of the Trinity the most withering criticism of which as an idealist philosopher he was capable. Dean Rashdall devoted much time in his later years to exposing its fallacy. Dr. F. R. Tennant of the University of Cambridge, one of the greatest philosophical theologians so far produced in this century, holds that there is no point of view intermediate between Monarchianism (or Sabellianism) and Tritheism that can claim empirical or logical standing ground. He has put forward as a possible solution of the problem an ethicized Christian Tritheism, without committing himself personally to this speculation.

Where are we today with respect to some kind of ultimate construction and understanding of the doctrine of the Trinity? The issues are perhaps in clearer and sharper focus than for a good while. They involve a choice between three alternative interpretations or theories of the Trinity. The first is Sabellianism. It might be better to say essential Sabellianism. The time is by when any good purpose is served through muddying the stream of clear thinking by technical evasions of the charge of Sabellianism. It is easily possible to do this in the case of lines of thought that convey much that is meaningful and true about the nature of God, but that refrain from asserting a Trinity of persons, since the main trend of the Sabellian fragments in our possession indicates a temporal succession in the manifesting of the "persons" of the Father, the Son, and the Spirit. The heart of the Sabellian view is, however, not the side-issue of time and God, but the fundamental thesis that the Trinity is one of appearance or experience, not of the being of God.

The second possibility is a "modal" construction of the Trinity. (The word "modal" I coin so as to distinguish the view in question from "modalism," a synonym in the textbooks for "Sabellianism.") This is the doctrine to which the Cappadocians finally came and which is the main trunk of developed Eastern Trinitarian theory. It was transmitted to the West, perhaps as a modification of Sabellianism, and has existed in Trinitarian thought since Augustine as one among several elements of a less static and a more dynamic but more subtle and difficult conception.

A useful illustration of the modal notion is the standard tradition of Byzantine art with respect to the depiction of the Blessed Trinity. In marked contrast to the use of artists in the mediæval West, marked by a simple fidelity to the Bible, this tradition calls for three identical human figures, mature in countenance rather than old, with the middle figure identified by a cross. Gregory of Nazianzus uses the metaphor of "one mingling of light, as it were of three suns joined together." The point that these illustrations are meant to bring out is that there is one identical Divine being in point of internal content, but that this Being, God Himself, exists really and objectively in a threefold manner —as Father, as Son, and as Holy Spirit. Or, in the words of an eminent Professor of the University of Cambridge, the late Dr. J. F. Bethune-Baker, the "Catholic interpretation" of the Trinity is that of "one God existing permanently and eternally in three spheres of consciousness and activity; three modes, three forms, three persons: in the inner relations of the Divine life as well as in the outer relations of the Godhead to the world and to men."

There is much to be said for the modal view of the Trinity. It avoids both Sabellianism and Tritheism. It says clearly that the Trinity is not merely a matter of revelation as registered in our experience, but is of the nature of God. Further, the three Persons can rightly be seen as having particular and distinctive functions alike in creation and in redemption. They can be intelligibly thought of as the object of Christian worship and faith. For long I was persuaded that this construction of the doctrine of the Trinity was not only the one most decisively indicated by Christian tradition viewed as a whole, but also the wisest and soundest solution of the intellectual problem presented by this doctrine.

It now seems to me that this conclusion is of doubtful validity. The modal view has numerous strong features, but it has two grave and possibly fatal defects.

(1) It has no clear analogy in human experience. Man is a personality; he is the self-conscious union of feeling, intellect, and will; he is a being who desires and reasons. Here is a possible analogy to the being of God, especially if man be regarded, as by Christianity, as created in the image of God. Or man is a social being. Personality is a social pro-

duct, and lives and thrives only in a context of social relations. The human being may be egocentric to an extreme
degree, but even at the moment of his most intense egoism
he is the subject of other-regarding thoughts and desires.
Here, too, is a clear-cut analogy to the being of God, who
has thus created man. But of a God who is in some manner
plural, who is in His essence a Trinity of persons, and who
yet has within Himself no analogue of love, friendship,
communion of souls, we have no analogy, no hint, in things
human. This is perhaps the reason for the popularity, from
the days of the Christian Fathers down to the generality of
sermons preached on last Trinity Sunday, of impersonal
and material analogies such as the sun, its ray, and a sun-
beam; a fountain, a river, and a rivulet; water, ice, and
vapour; and all the complicated diagrams of traditional
Trinitarian symbolism.

(2) The modal view leans too heavily on the relation of
God to the world of creation (and redemption as a process
set within it). It contains nothing within it that is intrin-
sically self-explanatory and intellectually satisfying from
the standpoint of God-in-Himself. It is of course possible
that creation is eternal and that there is no reason to posit
a beginning (or presumably an end) of the world. This
was the view of Aristotle and of Origen. St. Thomas
Aquinas may have been prevented from espousing it only
by the authority of the Catholic Church. It was revived by
philosophical idealism in the nineteenth century. Modern
Anglican theologians like Temple and W. R. Matthews have
advocated it. The question is highly speculative. But there
is much evidence adduced by modern scientific experiment
and theory that is against an eternal creation (see Chapter
II and compare Sir James Jeans' *The Mysterious Universe* and
Sir Arthur Eddington's *The Nature of the Physical World*).
Christian orthodoxy, influenced no doubt mainly by the
Bible, is against it. And in any case the Christian doctrine
of creation is decisive in asserting that God is independent
of creation and in no way organic to it. If this be true, no
one can dismiss the question of the nature of God-in-
Himself, of the eternal and timeless essence and life of
Godhead, as meaningless or irrelevant or futile. It is the
most important question there is.

The third alternative in thought about the Trinity is the admission of the analogy of personal society, intercourse, and fellowship. It is the view that God within the unity of His Divine life experiences and comprehends communication, mutuality, love and shared beatitude. It is the conception set forth by St. Augustine in expounding St. John's assertion that "God is Love," but from which he shrank back, feeling, as it were, an excess of light, as he tried thus to think of God. Here he is wiser than many expositors of a social God in the late nineteenth and early twentieth centuries. We shall do well, if we embrace the third alternative, as I am persuaded we must to be truly and fully Christian in our thinking about God, to imitate the candour and theological modesty of the great Doctor and Bishop of Hippo.

In accepting and trying to state in terms that are valid for the Being of God the social analogy, great care must be taken to safeguard and to emphasize the ultimate and absolute unity of God. On this Christian tradition, following Holy Scripture, is adamant in firmness and unmistakable in clarity. There is, however, nothing in the Christian revelation that requires a unity conceived in terms of a mathematical abstraction. It so happened that classical theology was dominated by Greek modes of thought, which had been elaborated when mathematics was the supreme science. The analogy of a complex organism, animated by a single organizing principle or centre, but constituted out of diverse elements, is just as valid so far as the idea of unity is concerned, and is required if any sense is to be made of the conception of three Persons in one God. Professor Hodgson has advanced Trinitarian thought by insisting on this in his recent book, already cited.

In addition, and finally, we shall be helped, and a certain break, not with the orthodox dogma of the Trinity, but with the standard elaborations of it by the majority of classical theologians, will be cushioned if we keep in mind the position already sketched (in Chapters I and II) with respect to Christian doctrine and reason. This position, in brief, is that it is more reasonable to face and accept the fact that every resort to analogy in trying to think about God ends in symbolic and mythical representation than it is to pretend that pure reason yields valid and satisfactory conclusions in theology. Christianity stands at this point midway between the rationalism of Western philosophy in its main line and the self-conscious ideologism of Marxist thought and of the prevailing contemporary mentality. Applied to the doctrine of the Trinity, this means that the Christian facts, plus the logic of the highest and most satisfactory analogy which human experience yields, demand a realistic, dramatic, and mythological interpretation of the being and the relations of Father, Son, and Holy Spirit.

It remains to attempt a very simple statement of the doctrine of the Trinity. Taking our lead from Holy Scripture and from many passages in the ancient Fathers, we shall make this statement as concrete as possible. We shall give it the form of a description of the being of God as Trinity and Unity. Such a description will necessarily be in part a picture. And since God has given us only one portrait of Himself, and that in a mode adapted to our vision and understanding—namely, human flesh—our attempt at portraiture of Eternal Divinity will have to be done with the aid of imagination. But we have also and must use reason, working on the basis of (a) the Christian facts and (b) the principles and ideas worked out and tested through centuries of exact and exacting thought by Christian doctors and philosophers.

In the beginning God, called at divers times and with differing meanings "Father," created the heavens and the earth. But in this work of making worlds God the Father was not alone. With Him was the Logos (Word), and the Logos was God. Through the Logos, in whom dwelt perfectly as in an identical image the whole mind of God, were all things made (John i. 1-3).

With God, also, was His Spirit, identical with Him in knowledge, the searcher of "all things, yea, the deep things of God" (I Corinthians ii. 10), yet ever proceeding from Him and at the same time abiding with Him. Through the Spirit, also, were all things made. His it was to brood over the face of ancient waters and to give both energy to matter and breath to living things (Genesis i. 2).

In the beginning, then, was God the Father, and with

Him His Word or only begotten Son and the uncreated Divine Spirit. Not with the creation did this Trinity come into being; rather from before all beginnings and apart from all succession, timelessly and eternally, God was a Triune God. He was both One and Three. He was alone— the only, awful, invisible, unapproachable, inconceivable ground of all things and abyss of all being. Yet He was not alone—not blank existence, not an immovable, everlasting fixture, not a lifeless absolute or an impersonal structure of universal order. In Him, of His very essence as God, was life, motion, self-knowledge, self-communication, self-giving, love, bliss, beatitude. How could it be otherwise when, as the writer says, "At Thy right hand there is pleasure for evermore"?[1]

Whence arose these qualities, and how is it that God is within Himself not sheer unity but a complex and manifold being, the union and communion of three Divine persons? Such a question is very difficult. The answer, as Plato said long ago of the problem of the creation and generation of the world, is hard to come at, and indeed can only be given in the form of a likely story. Or, we might say, a fitting picture or representation. We have, however, with regard to the question of the eternal Trinity a long tradition of reflection and imaginative thought by men who worshipped and prayed to the God of whose nature and being they desired to form the best and truest conception that was possible.

As these men have taught us, and looking also ourselves at the Scriptures as well as using to the best of our ability our own minds, we may speak in this wise of the origin and nature of the Divine Trinity. God is in Himself thought and energy, knowledge and will, reason and love. But in Him these qualities exist not as attributes now active and then passive, as with us. They exist in Him in the fulness of perfect actuality, and this actuality gives rise to a plurality of persons within the being of the One God (or in the technical language of classical Trinitarianism a multiplicity of concrete individual determinations of the Divine essence or substance). God as personal, conscious subject knows Himself as object. This knowledge involves a bringing into

[1] Psalm xvi. 12.

existence or generation, from all eternity, of another—
a perfect or identical image of the Father, in which the
Father sees Himself, His own mind, and all truth, all beauty,
and all goodness. Yet this other is living and substantial.
It is a real Divine *alter ego*. Or, to put it another way, God,
in knowing Himself, utters or projects or begets Himself as
a distinct Divine person. This self-utterance of God is the
eternal Word or Son.

But God is also love. In Him, if we know what we are
saying, there is infinite desire, infinitely and perfectly satisfied. (For the benefit of any theologians who may read this
book such a statement is not incompatible with the essential
and distilled truth of the idea of the impassibility of God,
an idea designed to bring out the contrast between the
conditions of Divine life and the changes, chances, sufferings, and passions of mortal human life.) So in the uttering
of the Word, from which act we must try to think away time
and becoming as we know them, we are not dealing with
pure intellectual contemplation. Thinker and thought there
must be, but that the thought must be personal and sub-
stantive, we do not know. The generation of the Son occurs,
therefore because it is the nature of God as Love to communicate Himself. Simultaneously with this generation
there goes forth or proceeds from the same Divine subject
a burning and yet never-to-be-consumed fire of love. This
Godly *dilectio*, this Primal energy of spirit and motion of
will, is likewise not transient and a mere quality, as with us,
but is a subsistent Person—the eternal Spirit.

Such is the Holy Trinity so far as we can apprehend and
make real to our minds this Three-Personal God of Christian worship and faith. Within the unity of one God there
are three real and distinct Persons, three centres of consciousness, will, and activity. Each is a personal agent, fully
God. Yet each partakes of and has His being in the same
identical Godhead, and is constituted internally by the same
attributes and a common Divine consciousness. Thus there
is a real sharing, a genuine communion, an authentic love.
But the diversity is within a unity which in intensity and
completeness surpasses all human thought and imagination.

This means that the action of one Divine person is His
own and at the same time the work of the undivided Trinity.

The climax of this is seen in the Incarnation, which is of the Word, and hence is on a special sense a deed of the only Son of God. Yet it is also an act of the whole Trinity. The same applies to the sovereignty of the Father in history, the immanence of the Spirit in the Church, and the presence of Christ in the Holy Eucharist. St. Thomas Aquinas is right in the invocation of his Eucharist hymn:

> O Saving Victim, opening wide
> The gate of heaven to man below.

He is equally right in passing at once to the praise of the undivided and eternal Trinity.

> All praise and thanks to Thee ascend
> For evermore, blest One in Three.

We have to do at every point with the love of the blessed Trinity—love in action, love manifested to us—but love first of being, love that eternally is, and love in which there is a true participation and fellowship of three Divine persons—the Father, the Son, and the Holy Spirit.

Batter my heart, three person'd God: for, you
As yet but knocke, breathe, shine, and seeke to mend,
That I may rise, and stand, o'erthrow mee, and bend
Your force, to breake, blowe, burn and make me new.

JOHN DONNE.

Men's curiosity searches past and future
And clings to that dimension. But to apprehend
The point of intersection of the timeless
With time, is an occupation for the saint—
No occupation either, but something given
And taken, in a lifetime's death in love,
Ardour and selflessness and self-surrender.

T. S. ELIOT: *Four Quartets.*

Greek man never owed more than finite debt to his gods. But the
case is changed as soon as we admit the existence of an absolute good,
such as that defined by Christianity. Human desire, henceforth, stands
in the presence of an object such that it becomes quite impossible to
desire it for anything other than itself.

ETIENNE GILSON: *The Spirit of Mediæval Philosophy.*

When she felt the kill-weights crush
She told His name times-over three;
I suffer this, she said, *for Thee.*

.   .   .   .   .   .

She caught the crying of those Three,
The Immortals of the eternal ring,
The Utterer, Utterèd, Uttering,
And witness in her place would she.

GERARD MANLEY HOPKINS.

CHAPTER V

Devotion and the Trinity

IN Chapter II we analyzed at length the idea and the psychology of devotion. We tried to go behind the ordinary connotations of the word and to explore its roots in the nature of man. Our central conclusion was that desire or love is the strongest thing there is in human life and that, consequently, man's most fundamental problem is to come into fruitful contact with an object great enough, and also sufficiently attractive and compelling, to order and direct and intensify at a higher level his native loyalty and devotion.

Such an object, if it exist, manifestly must be a subject as well. It must be One who loves. It must be a living and loving Will. The central contention, or rather announcement and claim, of Christianity is that the God of the universe has by His own act and Word shown Himself to be, not principally power, though He is that, or chiefly knowledge and wisdom, though He is both, but essential and eternal Love. By this conviction, which is the Christian good news, the religion called by the name of Christ overcame in a very few centuries every other competing philosophy and religion and carved out a new channel for the stream of human history. By the same conviction this religion will overcome the present crisis and agony of mankind and will be hailed once again as the good news of a new age. For there can be, literally, no other news that is good.

In the third and fourth chapters we attempted to explore and to portray the manner and the implications of the revelation that God is Love. We studied the Trinitarian form of this revelation and its interconnection from the earliest times in the minds and hearts of those to whom it came in power, with the certainty that Father, Son, and Holy Spirit were not names but true Divine persons. Then we sought to answer as clearly and intelligibly, and at the same time as richly and fully and satisfactorily, as we could the question, What is the doctrine of the Trinity, and what is its connection with the good announcement of Christianity that the Creator and Monarch of the world is a God of Love?

In this chapter we are going to be concerned especially with devotion in its religious and Christian sense and with the relations (note the plural form) of the life of devotion and the doctrine of the Trinity. We shall begin by asking anew the question, What is devotion? Then we shall consider in the light of all that has now been said the relation of devotion to the Christian doctrine of the Triune God. Finally, moving backwards, we shall attempt to note some devotional involvements and applications of the fact that the God to whom we are related is a Trinity of Persons.

What is Christian devotion? What is the devotional life? Is it saying one's prayers? Is it the cultivation of a prayerful spirit for all one's hours and days? Is it reading the Bible? Is it reading what we commonly speak of as devotional literature—that is, writings that describe the experiences and set down the thoughts of saints and other people sincerely and deeply concerned with life in the Spirit?

Or is devotion primarily a matter of act—of the deed? Is it doing something with and to and in one's self, which must mean the body as well as the soul, since it is the teaching of Christianity as well as modern science and psychology that the human being is an indivisible whole, a single psychophysical entity? Is devotion, then, systematic and particularistic ascetic discipline? Is it the renunciation of things created by God and good in themselves for the love of God and the welfare of others and one's own highest and eternal good? Is it fasting? (The Prayer Book, contrary apparently to the understanding as well as the practice of a very large number of Episcopalians, clearly enjoins and assumes fasting and provides for the faithful—seven or eight pages before the Order for Daily Morning Prayer—a Table of Fasts. It does not say anything about eating fish.) Is it giving alms, directly to those in need, or more intelligently and beneficially, often, through the community chest? Is it supporting liberally and at some personal sacrifice the Church and the mission of the Church throughout the nation and the world? Or is the real thing in devotion acting with other Christians and men of good will to gain through laws and the planning authorized by them a wider measure of justice and equality?

The answer in every case is obviously, Yes. But it is first

and very peremptorily, No. It is necessary to dig down deeper if we would know the meaning and the structure and the marks of true devotion. Devotion is above all devotedness of self. It is feeling within one's being the reality and knowing within one's will the force of

> that devotedness, in short,
> Which I account the ultimate in man;

and it is the perpetual direction and offering of this devotedness to God.

Devotion, being native and universal as an impulsion and spring of human action, is of various kinds and degrees. There is the devotion that is based upon instinct or passion. This is the most elemental and the most nearly universal form of devotedness. It is the primal, visible focus of the eternal desire that as the Breath of God moves in the whole creation; and it is a fountain of all spiritual creativity as well as the source of physical procreation and the instrument of the perpetuation of the species. At the same time it is the most imperious aspect of human dynamism and the most demonic and destructive in potentiality. Also, far from being a straightforward, simple affair of physics or endocrine chemistry, the impulse of sex is an exceptionally intricate psychological complex (or group of associated mental and emotive elements), including within its scope the relations and reactions of parents and children in a number of permutations and combinations as well as what is normally thought of as human sexuality.

At the opposite pole there is devotion to an abstract conviction, as, for example, the loyalty of a scientist to truth, or of an artist to beauty, or of a plain man to liberty. In between there is devotion to country, or patriotism, and devotion between persons as persons, or friendship. Lastly, there is religious devotion. It is the most inclusive. It is prefigured in all the rest. Psychologically, indeed, religion may be regarded as devotion itself in an intense, exalted, and comparatively durable form.

Thus every kind of devotion may assume a religious aspect. It may itself become a kind of religion. This is the truth in the philosopher Bosanquet's assertion that "wherever a man is so carried beyond himself, whether for any

other being, or for a cause or for a nation, that his personal
fate seems nothing in comparison with the happiness or
triumph of the other, there you have the universal basis and
structure of religion." John Keats, mystical devotee and
high priest of Beauty though he was, was so carried away
by a human love that he could write Fanny Brawne, "Love
is my creed, and you are its only tenet." A modern chau-
vinist could say, "Patriotism is my religion."[1] Will-worship,[2]
expressed in the virtual deification of leaders and the absolu-
tizing of particular nations and races, and bringing forth in
countless individuals an utter surrender of self, is now one
of the most familiar phenomena of modern history.

Normally, however, religion is directed beyond all
human and finite beings, institutions, and values. It is
directed toward something "not of this world." As against
Whitehead ("Religion is world loyalty") and Royce ("In
being loyal to universal loyalty we are serving the . . .
unity of the world-life"), it is in its distinctive and typical
manifestations oriented toward the holy (or separated),
the superhuman and supernatural, the transcendent, the
eternal, the Divine—God. Religion is devotion to God
conceived of as the Supreme Real. Its history reveals numerous variations in the idea of God. But it is very constant in
disclosing a tendency both to make God absolute and in
some way to personalize Him. (We are, of course, not
speaking of philosophy.)

Historical Buddhism is an instructive example. The point
of view of its founder Gautama or Sakyamuni the Buddha
seems to have been that of a humanist (in the modern religious sense). He abjured metaphysics and theology.
Nirvana, or the salvation which he discovered, is the conclusion of a chain of reasoning that issues out of a profound
and radical psychological analysis. To this the Buddha
added compassion, which moved him to defer Nirvana and
live on for others, so that as the late Canon B. H. Streeter
once said: "Buddhism sprang from Sakyamuni's consent
to live, Christianity from Christ's consent to die." But

---

[1] I have not been able to identify the author of this sentence, but I do not think
I have invented it. Citizen Tom Paine in the eighteenth century said, "My country
is the world"; and Guy de Maupassant wrote in a short story: "Patriotism is a kind
of religion. It is the egg from which wars are hatched."

[2] Colossians ii. 23.

Buddhism made its way as a world religion by metaphysics and by devotion to a deified Buddha—or, perhaps
better, to a Brahman Absolute invested with Buddhahood
and able to incarnate itself in numberless Buddhas.

Of historic Christianity it is a truism to say that its magnetic centre of attraction from the beginning has been the
figure of the Divine-human Christ as apprehended by the
first Christians and as portrayed in the New Testament.
This figure is that of a human personality—a man. This is
taken for granted by all writers of the New Testament. But
we have no record, and no sure evidence of the existence
even, of a Jesus who is not also "Christ"—an object of
faith related in a unique manner to the Father-God of Israel
and Monarch Absolute of the world. Here there is a vast
difference between Christianity and Buddhism. But there is
a parallel between them in the light which each throws on
the nature of religion and religious devotion. For, within
the Christian orbit, it is not as the One high and lifted up,
infinitely exalted above things human, but as the suffering
Son upon His freely chosen Cross, that God has reconciled
the world and freely won the love of human souls. And it
is as the risen Lord, *Christus Victor*, alive for evermore and
having in His hands the keys of death and Hades, that God
has made Himself known certainly and has enabled His
human creatures and children to cleave to Him with an
invincible love and an unfaltering trust.

There is in the Gospel according to St. John a remarkable surmise and prophecy of what has in fact come to pass.
"And I, if I be lifted up from the earth, will draw all men
unto Me."[1] This is the equivalent in terms of human and
religious psychology of the words of the risen Christ according to St. Matthew: "All authority is given unto Me."[2]
So it has proven throughout all Christian history. Christianity, it has been said, is the experience of belonging to
Jesus Christ. This is true, and will remain true. He it is who
among all historical figures has shown the power to attract
and hold the devotion of men.

There is in this inherent Christocentric bent of Christianity a definite danger. So it is with all good and great
things. Every virtue is liable to a special corruption, and

[1] xii. 32.   [2] xxviii. 18.

pre-eminent excellence or strength or beauty most of all. The special peril of Christianity is Jesuolatry, or the worship of Jesus either as a creature or in a creaturely aspect separated from its true context or exaggerated to the point of monstrous disproportion. It is illustrated in almost every period of Church history and in all types of Christian piety. It was a threat to the primitive Church, manifest especially in its cultus, as it broke away from the moorings of institutional Judaism and was exposed to the violent and world-wide spiritual wave of mystery religion. Even with the victory over Gnosticism and Marcionism (in both of which incidentally the Christian element is Christ cut sharply out of His historical context, past and immediate) Jesuolatry was not overcome, but assumed a philosophical guise in the concept of the Logos, who tended not only to relegate the Father to a position of unconditioned untouchability, but to leave the Spirit of God no distinctive functions. (See above, Chapter III.) Coming closer to our time, the same tendency may be seen in popular Catholicism, with its morbid exaggeration of the agony of Christ and its unbalanced exaltation of the sacred humanity in varied particular aspects. It can be seen equally clearly (and the parallel here is surely arresting) in sectarian Protestantism, with its garish realism of "the fountain filled with blood" and doctrine of reconciliation only through the application to the sin-spotted soul of the atoning blood of Christ. (Anglicans, in particular, should not forget the influence upon this phase of Protestant religion of the doctrine and the hymnody of the eighteenth century Anglican Evangelicals.) Last, but not least, there is liberal Christianity (or perhaps more accurately, Christian Liberalism), with its reduction of Christ to the status of a rabbi adopted as the special human son of the Heavenly Father, or the more equivocal statement that Jesus has the value of God. Yet no other major type of Christianity has gone so far in limiting our knowledge of God entirely and absolutely to Jesus Christ.

These trends are matters of fact. They are not set down with a polemical intent, but rather sympathetically as well as critically (from a final standpoint). What they actually do is to bear witness powerfully to the pre-eminence of the

figure of Jesus Christ and to the special strength and appeal
of Christianity as the religion of the Incarnation. But the
mere recital of these trends, together with the recognition
immediately given with the recital of their bearing upon
the nature of devotion, underlines the importance of cease-
lessly reiterating the saying of the second century letter
known as Second Clement:

> Brethren, we must think of Jesus Christ as of God. . . . For he gave
> us the light, he called us "son", as a Father, he saved us when we were
> perishing.

This is a kind of motto of classical Christology (= ordered
thought about Jesus Christ). But it soon appeared, as it
still appears after careful reflection, that the ascription of
full deity as well as humanity to Christ is not enough. For
what is His relation, then, to the Father? Who is the
Divine Word that personally became flesh and lives and
spoke and died, not as a man merely, but as a God? Was it
Rousseau who, pagan as he was in many respects and rebel
against the Christian tradition, confessed: "The life and
death of Socrates were those of a philosopher; the life and
death of Jesus were those of a God"? The same general
comparison, appropriately rephrased, might, I believe, be
made of the Buddha (or Enlightened One) and the Christ.
So we reach the necessity of the kind of theological
thinking that we call Trinitarian. We perceive the reason
for the doctrine of the Trinity. It is important philosophically: it points us beyond religious experience to ultimate
and perfect, to unmoved-moved being. It is important
theologically: it points us to the reality and Godhead of the
Father and of the Holy Spirit, God above us and God
within us, as well as to the Divinity of Jesus Christ.[1] It is
important devotionally: it points us to the infinite majesty
and unapproachable holiness and otherness or God, before
whom, as it was revealed to Abraham before Christ or even
before Moses, we human creatures are "but dust and ashes,"[2]
and to the reality of a power not ourselves that can work in
us invisibly and secretly to do the will of God, as well as to
"the grace of our Lord Jesus Christ," manifest in obedience

[1] *Cf.* Romans xi. 36: "For of Him, and through Him, and unto Him, are all things."
[2] Genesis xviii. 27.

as of a Son and in willingness out of pure yet passionate love to offer His life for sinners.

But we must return to the central point still under consideration—namely, the meaning of religious and Christian devotion. Religious devotion is, then, self-surrender. It is a love so great that one is moved to take up one's very life and lay it on some altar, whether it be that of human passion, of family loyalty, of patriotism, of reverence for truth, of the sentiment of humanity, or of the adoration of God. Christianity is clear that it is the last, and the last only, that can be properly called religious. It teaches that the life of true devotion is the life dedicated and actually devoted to God. Devotion is the love of Him "with all thy heart, and with all thy soul, and with all thy mind":[1] it is willing the will of God, not for one's own ends or even to gain other ends that may seem and may be very good and very precious, but for the sake of God.

The Lord's Prayer is decisive on this point. With a simplicity that only Incarnate God could have achieved, our Lord teaches us to say, when we pray: (1) Thy name be hallowed; (2) Thy kingdom come; (3) Thy will be done, as in heaven so on earth. Then, but only then, we are to pray, (4) for bread—surely a symbol for the basic material necessities of life; (5) for the forgiveness of sins (the daily bread—and one might truly add, bath—of the soul); and (6) for deliverance from evil (regarded—how rightly!—as something active, and menacing, and threatening constantly our lives as individual spirits and as social beings: the correct translation may be "the Evil One"). The first three petitions illustrate the primacy and the Godward direction of Christian devotion; the last three express our dependence on God and our obligation in the spirit of love to our fellow-men (*our daily bread . . . as we forgive . . . lead us not . . . deliver us*).

But Christianity has more than this prayer, which is indeed not so much a particular prayer as prayer itself—the perfection and essence of all prayer. It has also at its centre a life—the life of Christ. This life is the supreme example from first to last of a devotedness that knew no inward contradiction and that reveals no seam or trace of fracture and

[1] Matthew xxii. 37.

awkward subsequent jointure. It is like the coat or tunic worn by our Lord at the time of His crucifixion, spoken of in the Gospel according to St. John, perhaps with a conscious realization of something profoundly symbolic, as "without seam, woven from the top throughout," and so attractive that the soldiers elected to cast lots for it rather than to "rend it" and divide the pieces of cloth.[1] Or, we might say, applying in a more eminent and superlative manner to Origen's Lord, the words that were said of the great scholar, exegete, theologian, and Christian philosopher of ancient Alexandria: his life was "one unbroken prayer."

Christian devotion is union with the life of Christ in the power of the Holy Spirit. This is the inward meaning of Holy Baptism, in which we are baptized into a new life, reborn into Christ in the one Spirit. "If any man be in Christ, there is a new creation."[2] But life is not static. It is growth, change, development. Baptism is a beginning. But one has to learn and grow into faith, love, and a sense of the fact and meaning for life of the Holy Spirit. Confirmation, or the laying on of hands upon a baptized person, is an outward and visible sign, which is not simply a sign, but also an effectual instrument, of receiving the Spirit and with Him the choice gifts of the love and grace of God. It is not only the sign or means, although it is Scriptural (Acts viii. 14-18; xix. 1-7), and it has in its favour, in addition, both ancient, continuous tradition and pragmatic psychological effectiveness. With the Holy Communion it is the same, only more so. There are, according to the Catechism of the Book of Common Prayer, two Sacraments "ordained by Christ in His Church," and "two only, as generally necessary to salvation; that is to say, Baptism and the Supper of the Lord."

The second great Sacrament, or Holy Communion, is the special sign and means of growth and renewal in the Christian life. It is also above all the Sacrament of Devotion, as we have analyzed and defined it. As we "make" "the memorial" suggested and, we believe, commanded by Christ Himself, re-enacting mystically and symbolically His death, trying to think and feel as though the sacrifice of the

---

[1] xix. 23-24.   [2] 2 Corinthians v. 17.

Lamb without blemish were now taking place, and as we then receive the bread and drink of the cup blessed by Him and called with His own lips "My Body" and "My Blood," we receive Him, the only and the perfect Son, into ourselves: we are made one Body with Him and are made partakers through Him, in the unity and the life-giving power of the Spirit, of the life and love of the holy and undivided Trinity.

For us, on our part, this involves not only worship and faith and humility (or poverty of spirit realized and accepted in simplicity) and obedience, or even praise and thanksgiving, but devotion and love: the love that carries in its hands life-blood and life-energy and a will to uncalculating sacrifice and giving of self. Rightly, as the Canon in the Communion Service of the American Book of Common Prayer nears its close, in a kind of fourth movement, as it were, of a Divine symphony, the Priest, speaking for the people as for himself, says:

And here we offer and present unto thee, O Lord, our selves, our souls and bodies, to be a reasonable, holy, and living sacrifice unto thee.

The same point is illustrated in prayer. Prayer is offered by human beings, and springs out of the common needs and desires and hopes and aspirations of humanity. It wells out initially from the situation of a man's existence. This is fully recognized and amply illustrated in the Bible. The Psalter, called by John Donne "the manna of the Church," contains a series of prayers of this order. It is full of petitions like those that went up from men stranded for many days in rubber lifeboats in the Pacific and knowing that they had no power even to get food enough or water enough to maintain life. Christ also, again with a simplicity that is the mark of God, recognized this element in prayer and called on men to pray with persistent importunity and unquestioning faith. Yet if Christian devotion is union with the life of Christ, prayer cannot stop with petition that grows out of human and natural desires and hopes. Such prayer by itself is like Christianity without the Cross. It is human but not Divine—not fully and maturely of the Holy Spirit who knows not only "the deep things of God"[1] but is the searcher of all the hearts, and who out of His love and knowledge and sympathy for human infirmity "makes intercession for us with groanings which cannot be uttered."[2] No, the ultimate prayer, and the final characteristic of Christian devotion, is the spirit like unto that of our Lord in the Garden of Gethsemane. Our human, finite, anxious, restless, grasping, insatiable will is surrendered—surrendered joyfully if in mortal anguish and agony, and surrendered unquestioningly, for the perfect will of God.

Abba, Father, all things are possible unto thee; take away this cup from me: nevertheless not what I will, but what thou wilt.[3]

It is not different with fasting and all self-discipline and self-denial. It is the same, also, with giving of money or goods and with loving and serving our neighbour. It is as these acts express the central bent of the will organized around the master motive of love toward God and loyalty to His kingdom that they are properly acts of Christian devotion and are of value in God's sight. St. Paul saw this with great clarity, and outlined by implication both a Christian psychology of the will and an acute strategy of the devotional life when he wrote:

And though I . . . understand all mysteries, and all knowledge; and though I have faith, so that I could remove mountains, and have not love, I am nothing. And though I bestow all my goods to feed the poor, and though I give my body to be burned and have not love, it profiteth me nothing.[4]

It is only as there is love in our hearts which is in little the reflection of the *agape* of God, the Divine love which goes out to search for sinners and does not swerve from sacrifice, that we have within us the love of Christ and that we are in the Spirit. This love, of which St. Paul speaks, cannot be divided neatly into love for God and love for man. It is one love, directed toward God primarily, but in its movement toward Him intersecting and including our fellow-men, who are as much as we the object of the Divine *agape*. St. Augustine, and after him Peter the Lombard, the Master of the *Sentences* and teacher of the whole of mediæval

---

[1] I Corinthians ii. 10.
[3] Mark xiv. 36.
[2] Romans viii. 26.
[4] I Corinthians xiii. 2-3.

Christendom, got hold of this principle and gave it a final statement. "The love wherewith a man loves God and his neighbour is the Holy Ghost." Martin Luther, who as an Augustinian monk and theological professor had lectured on the *Sentences*, saw this principle clearly. But under the influence of a living rediscovery of the Word of God as it came through Christ and St. Paul and St. Peter, he felt and expressed with a novel depth and penetration of insight the meaning for human relations of the mysterious *agape* or love of God.

But love is greater than brotherhood, for it extends even to our enemies, and especially to those who are not worthy of love. For as faith performs its work where it sees nothing, so also should love see nothing, and there especially exercise its office where there appears nothing lovely, but only disaffection and hostility. Where there is nothing that pleases me, I should the more seek to be pleased. And this spirit should go forth fervently, says St. Peter, just as God loved us when we were not worthy of love.[1]

This, as is obvious to anyone, is a large order. It is a view of human destiny that cuts deeply. It runs squarely against stubborn cross-currents in human nature—in the nature of which we all partake. And Christianity, oddly enough, recognizes this. It recognizes and expounds it and drives it home and warns with regard to it in the most realistic and radical way conceivable. The Bible is far from being a pretty or a nice book. Not Shakespeare himself holds the mirror up to the nature of man so steadily or in a light so intense and keen. Christianity is at once the most humanist and anti-humanist of all religions. In support of the anti-humanist or pessimistic pole of the Christian outlook one need only cite, leaving aside the realism of the concrete portrayals of actual men and women in Old Testament "History" beginning with Genesis, Matthew vii. 13-14, Mark vii. 17-23, Romans i. and vii., Colossians iii. 5-11, Ephesians iv. 17-24, James iii., 1 John ii. 15, and 2 Timothy iii. 1-9. If these passages stood alone, it would have to be said that no more sombre and unrelieved description of the human situation had ever been penned. The later doctrines of Original Sin and the Fall are not alien importations into the Bible; they represent an attempt at description and explana-

[1] Commentary on Peter and Jude.

tion on the basis of the Bible in the further confirmatory
light of observation and experience.

Yet the fact is that Christianity is far from being pessimistic about man. It is optimistic and expectant. The final
impression the New Testament leaves is not one of gloom
and tragedy, but of confidence and victory. And this impression comes out of vibrant, bracing experience, not out
of the existence of a message that sounds promising and
would appear to be worth exploration, but that has yet to
be put to the acid test of faith and practice. It comes out of
the lives of devoted and transformed men and women.

This was in accordance with the expectation of Christ
Himself. He called on His disciples to offer themselves to
God as He had done. He called on them to follow Him in
self-denial, obedience, love, and the way of the Cross. He
clearly supposed that they would find the power to do it.
He planned His own death, not so precisely as such words
suggest, for He had to take one step at a time and feel His
way, and our evidence suggests that the desire to live was
strong in Him and until after Gethsemane never ceased to
stab and tear within His human will. Yet He decided definitely to die, seeing that this was the one thing men could
never forget, discerning that this was the one way to show
them the meaning of Divine love and to propel them by its
energy along the same path that He had travelled and was
to travel to the end.

It is not different with us or other men and women in the
twentieth century. Human nature has not changed at all.
This has come as a shock to most people, who supposed
that we were somehow more enlightened and inherently
more progressive and developed than the ancients or
especially provincial folk with a mediæval mind. Yet nothing
is more surely the verdict of the history of our century to
date. "Mankind is for ever advancing, but man ever remains the same."

But this fact has a two-edged application. If it means
that man is as potentially wicked, godless, inhuman, fool-
ishly vain, blindly corrupt, and devilishly sensual and
proud as he ever was, it also means that he is still created
in the image of God and that he is as capable now of having
that image vivified and repaired through Jesus Christ, the

8

perfect image of the Father, as he was then. He is as capable of bringing forth the fruit of the Spirit (Galatians v. 22-23) as he ever was. So the question that confronts us as we think about the devotional life, which is a life united with Christ's, a will moved to firm juncture with the will of God, is still basically the question of motive. The problem is to find an impelling desire, a dynamic inward motion, a spiritual current strong enough to overcome all contrary forces, all downward suctions, all counter-tides, all fierce waves, and to bear our lives Godward in the way of Jesus Christ. It is to discover, or to allow something or someone to create in us, an affection and an interest so powerful that it becomes the centre of our lives and the pivot of all "the desires of our wills."

Where can we find such a motive? In one direction and from one source, and one only. The direction is the vision of God in the perfection of His eternal being and beauty. The source is living encounter with God the blessed Trinity, a God who has acted and ever acts in love because He is within Himself, eternally, the ground, the actuality, and the perfection of all love. The two things, vision and encounter, are not opposed but complementary. There is bound to be, in the life of Christian devotion, a continual interplay between them. It is only as we see, and our seeing is made vivid and compelling through imagination, that we shall meet and experience. It is only as we experience, in the thrust and outreach and also in the receptivities of our existence, feeling with an indefinable but undoubted certainty that our hearts are known[1] and our will mysteriously energized, that our vision and thought of God will be enlarged and clarified, and become a source of unending joy and impenetrable peace. "This is life eternal, that they should know Thee the only true God, and Jesus Christ, whom Thou didst send."[2] "Bless us, O God, with the vision of Thy Being and Beauty, that in the strength of it we may work without haste and without rest; through Jesus Christ our Lord."[3]

The doctrine of the Trinity represents in our knowledge

---

[1] *Cf.* 1 Corinthians xii. 12. [2] John xvii. 3.
[3] A prayer of the late Professor Henry Sylvester Nash of the Episcopal Theological School.

of God the union of the two great complements of Christian experience: vision and encounter. In the order of logic and perhaps of normal present-day experience, given not only the New Testament but the tradition of the Church, vision comes first. This vision is of God, who is Three yet One, who is Trinity in Unity and Unity in Trinity. The reason for thus speaking of the logical precedence of the vision of God is that being precedes action in a nature that is fully determined and therefore unchangeable and eternal. The heart of the Christian vision of God is the reality of Three "dwelling in the light which no man can approach unto,"[1] yet made known to us by God's own self-revelation as Father, Son, and Holy Spirit. Accordingly, as one tries to gaze with Dante

> In that abyss
> Of radiance, clear and lofty, seem'd methought,
> Three orbs of triple hue, clipt in one bound:
> And, from another, one reflected seem'd,
> As rainbow is from rainbow: and the third
> Seem'd fire, breathed equally from both."[2]

Or, turning from the pure imagery of poetry to the sober analogies of thought set down in prose, God is not a single, rigidly unitary being. He is not simply the Father. From all eternity He has put forth or generated as an object of knowledge and love His Word or only Son and perfect identical image, the sharer of the whole mind of God. In the process of uttering or generating by way of thought and because of love the Son there proceeds simultaneously and eternally by way of will an infinite Spirit of love who is the bond of union and communion of both. In this communion of one Spirit, the Father and the Son together with the same Spirit, a subsistent Person also, and a sharer of the whole mind of Godhead, enjoy an ineffable fellowship. They experience eternally the fruition of love in its perfection, along with all other graces and excellences possessed and tasted in little by us who have been created in the Divine image. Yet this triune God is one being, one complex three, personal Divine organism, if we may express ourselves so daringly, after the example of no less rational and philosophical a theologian than Aristotle, who was not afraid to speak of

---

[1] 1 Timothy vi. 16.   [2] *Paradise, Divine Comedy.*

the eternal Thinker as an animal or animated being, a
ξῷον.

In the order, however, of history and of original experience encounter precedes vision. In a real sense it does
still in every person's recapitulation within himself of the
history of revelation. At least vision will have no great
meaning without an encounter with the God who is known
as knowledge and love because of Jesus Christ and because
of the Holy Ghost. It is in the Cross that we know that God
is verily our Father and that we are sons and heirs of a
matchless inheritance. It is in the power of the Holy Spirit
that we know certainly that the crucified rabbi Jesus is Very
God and Lord of History, and that His love for us is the
love of God Himself. And it is by the operation of the
Spirit that we are born into a knowledge of the greatness
and ultimacy of the love that finds its nature and glory
realized in sacrifice and self-forgetfulness. So the Christian
encounter ends with vision—the vision of God the Blessed
Trinity, whose nature and whose name is Love.[1]

It remains to consider in a direct and quite concrete way
the relation of the doctrine of the Trinity to the practice of
the life of devotion. If God is, as Christians believe, Triune
—if He is Father, Son, and Holy Spirit bound together in
an essential and perfect unity—how should this affect our
approach to religion conceived of as a relation between the
soul and God, which is what we mean by the devotional
aspect of religion?

That a definite effect should be registered is evident.
Any view of God or the Supreme Real affects practice by an
inherent necessity. It affects not simply conduct or actual
deeds among men, but emotional and spiritual being—the
inward attitude, disposition, and varied reactions of a given
individual consciousness. A superb illustration of this is the
character of Anselmo in Ernest Hemingway's novel *For
Whom the Bell Tolls*. Anselmo is all out for the Spanish

---

[1] *Cf.* Charles Wesley's hymn beginning "Come, O Thou Traveller unknown",
and containing in the last stanza of the version used in the authorized Episcopalian
Hymnal of 1916 (since replaced officially by that of 1940) the lines:

'Tis Love! 'Tis Love! Thou diedst for me!
. . . . . .
Pure, universal Love Thou art;
To me, to all, Thy mercies move;
Thy nature and Thy name is Love.

Republic. But, as he stands on guard in the cold, he worries about the killing that has been done. There will have to be after the war, he thinks, "some great penance done for the killings. If we no longer have religion after the war I think there must be some form of civic penance organized that all may be cleansed from the killing or else we will never have a true and human basis for living." "Then he stood there against the tree stamping his feet softly and he did not think any more about the bridge. The coming of the dark always made him feel lonely and tonight he felt so lonely that there was a hollowness in him as of hunger. In the old days he could help this loneliness by the saying of prayers and often coming home from hunting he would repeat a great number of the same prayer and it made him feel better. But he had not prayed once since the movement. He missed the prayers, but he thought it would be unfair and hypocritical to say them and he did not wish to ask any favours or for any different treatment than all the men were receiving."

In a similar, if reversed, manner the person who really believes in the Divine Trinity is bound to be affected in his thought, feeling, praying, reading, and basic response to life. No one could predict, and no one would wish to try to plot, the shape or quality of such an effect in the case of any individual person. Since, however, devotion is a combined art and science with a long tradition, in the course of which certain definite principles have been evolved, it is fitting as a conclusion to this chapter to note and summarize some of the implications of the doctrine of the Trinity for what may be conveniently called the tactics of the devotional life. The strategy we have covered: it emerges from the nature of devotion and the consequent necessity for an object sufficiently compelling and powerful to move and transform our wills. This object is the Trinitarian God, revealed in history and experience as a God who loves the world and wills to save it because He is in Himself, essentially and eternally, Love. As it is love that moves the human will, and as love is begotten only by perceived value or by being loved, or more likely by the two in combination, so a God or Supreme Real, absolute in being, embodying all beauty, truth, and justice, who is at the same time Love, is able to impart to human nature what nothing else can—a motive-power able to remake and transform our natural wills.

We proceed now to set down concisely under definite heads some practical devotional implications of the doctrine of the Trinity. But we should never in working on special tactical problems lose sight of the master strategy. The two go together in the Christian warfare as much as in specialized military science.

1. MEDITATION

Meditation is the art of conforming our wills to God by means of deliberate mental concentration and direction of imagination. A good analogy to meditation is the daily practice of the distance runner on the track or across country, as distinct from the more negative aspects of his training, such as abstaining from certain food and drink and avoiding late hours. Meditation is the deliberate, regular, systematic practice of the presence of God through thinking about Him, letting one's imagination dwell upon Him, and recalling all that He has done in creation, redemption, and sanctification.

The doctrine of the Trinity states the Christian view of the being of God based upon the Divine action and speech (or word) in history as recorded and interpreted in the Bible. It is at once the supreme theme of meditation and the summary of nearly all important secondary subjects of meditation. The favourite theme of meditation is, perhaps, the figure of our Lord in some aspect of His life, passion, death, and resurrection. Without suggesting any detraction of this well-established custom based upon a deep instinct, since, after all, as we have urged above, the figure of Christ has always been the magnetic centre of Christianity, and since the Trinity is itself the outcome of the faith of the Incarnation, I believe, nevertheless, that meditation would gain in depth and force if we were to concentrate habitually, not on our Lord merely, but on the Father, the Son, and the Holy Spirit, in their mutual relations and their absolute and ultimate oneness. In this connection I may refer to the conclusion of Chapter IV, which is a kind of meditation

P. 98

upon the Trinitarian God in which reason and the imagination march together.

In addition, there is endless scope for meditation upon the Persons of the Trinity severally and upon their deeds and functions as set forth in Scripture and worked out more maturely in the developed Trinitarian aspect of Christian tradition. Two subjects occur to me as suggestive and illustrative: "the Atonement as a Deed of God" and "the Holy Spirit as the Secret Ally and Armourer of the Soul." But in all such meditations the Trinitarian background and point of ultimate rest in the interpretation of Christian truth should not be lost sight of.

2. THE BIBLE

There are various ways of reading the Bible. Today the fashion is to advocate reading it as living literature. How effective this has been in stemming a mounting tide of Biblical illiteracy and promoting a wider knowledge of the content of the Bible is a matter on which little if any data is available. Prior to the advent of the so-called "higher criticism" about a century ago, and the eventual discovery even by the plain man that there was a human and fallible side to the Bible, it was generally read as a collection of Divine oracles. It was read, not because it was interesting or curious or elevating or profound, but because it was believed to be throughout, uniformly and verbally, the Word of God.

This is not the place to enter into the question of the literary, psychological and humane value of the Bible. Mr. George Bernard Shaw is reported to have said, several years back, that "a great deal of the Bible is much more alive than the morning newspaper and last night's Parliamentary debate. Its chronicles are better reading than most of our fashionable histories and less intentionally mendacious. In revolutionary invective and utopian aspiration it cuts the ground from under the feet of Ruskin, Carlyle, and Karl Marx, and in the epoch of great leaders and great rascals it makes Homer seem superficial and Shakespeare unbalanced." All of which may be true. It is true also that the King James version is the most precious single item in the literary heritage of the English-speaking peoples.

There is no way in which to measure its influence upon the English language and English literature.

But none of these things is of supreme moment when we assess the significance of the Bible for Christian faith and Christian devotion. The important thing about the Bible is not what it says of man *per se*, however true and profound. The unique and really weighty feature of the Bible is that it is the book, and the one book, in which God is the chief character—in which He acts and speaks to communicate to men that which otherwise they could not and would not know. For the Christian, therefore, nothing can replace reading the Bible with a view to hearing in and through it the Word of God as a Divine Contemporary to our hearts, minds, and wills. The reading of the Bible from this standpoint must take first place along with prayer in the Christian devotional life.

For a fruitful reading of the Holy Scripture in our day there are several requisites. One is intelligence. The Christian must try to bring to this reading at least as sound a judgment and as thorough a preparation as he would bring to any other important study. This will include securing and using the best aids available—not highly technical works of criticism, but informed and constructive introductions and general commentaries. It will involve planned reading. The old custom or method, in vogue in my mother's youth and young womanhood, of reading the entire Bible through annually by the practice of reading three chapters every week-day and five every Sunday has gone never to return. No one today would equate in importance Leviticus and Isaiah. Yet there is a danger, at least in America, that public reading of the Old Testament will become largely confined to the prophets and wisdom literature (and the Psalter), to the comparative exclusion of the historical books.

Another requisite is reverent expectation. Here there is a close connection between Bible reading and prayer. We should expect that God will speak to us, as well as we to Him, and that, normally, He will do this not so much by putting thoughts into our minds out of the blue as by addressing us through the deeds and words and thoughts set down under Divine inspiration in the Bible. A third requisite is the faithful and persistent invocation of the Holy Spirit. Such invocation should normally be made at both the beginning and end of any period, however short, of reading and studying the Bible. Revelation is not really given until it is received. It is always a contemporary transaction, and it is the Holy Spirit, the Lord and Giver of Life, who presides over the proceeding. He it is who enables the seeking Christian to find that his reverent musing and listening and pondering have their fruit in a kindling of fire. But the Spirit does not work in a vacuum. His mission is not an unrelated and independent Divine undertaking. He is one of an indivisible Divine Trinity, and it is His task to take the things of the Father declared and wrought in deed by the eternal Word made flesh. "But when the Comforter is come, whom I will send unto you from the Father, even the Spirit of truth, which proceedeth from the Father, He shall bear witness of Me . . . for He shall not speak from Himself; but what things soever He shall hear, these shall He speak."[1]

3. PRAYER

The meaning of prayer for the life of devotion has already been touched on in this chapter. Here we shall deal simply and specifically with aspects or problems of prayer connected with the doctrine of the Trinity.

Christian prayer is ordinarily addressed to God as God or, adapting some words of the Trinity Sunday Collect, to God in the Unity of His Divine Majesty. Such address customarily takes one of two main forms: "Almighty God" and "Father" or "Our Father." The Book of Common Prayer, which of course reflects in general the Latin liturgical tradition, illustrates the first form of Divine salutation, with a number of significant and interesting variations, such as "Almighty and most merciful Father" (General Confession) and "Almighty God, Father of all mercies" (General Thanksgiving). American Protestantism, so far as it retains among its primary institutions *ex tempore* prayer, is wedded almost universally to "Father," with very minor variations, and with the substitution on occasion of "God" or "O God."

[1] John xv. 26; xvi. 13.

Each tradition has its special strength, and there is no point in tarrying to analyze further. In either case it is to God in His unity, God as Lord and Father, that we habitually pray, and this will and ought to remain normative. The equally normative ending for the Book of Common Prayer, again following very ancient tradition long maintained, of "through Jesus Christ our Lord," has much to commend it. This use as a whole has won and maintained its place (a) because of convenience; (b) because of the mediatorial significance of the Incarnation (it is as man, according to 1 Timothy and Hebrews, that Christ is mediator and high priest—a view that became traditional); and (c) because of the doctrine of the Trinity (which preserves the idea of one God at the same time that it asserts His self-revelation and the fulness of the Divine personal life out of which it comes in all its relative plurality).

If, however, the doctrine of the Trinity is true, there is ample warrant for the address of prayer to the several Persons of the Trinity and to the Trinity itself. Here Cranmer has shown the way in his Litany and also in the too little known prayer which he had written out before his final trial, and which he prayed as he knelt on the specially erected platform in St. Mary's, Oxford, just before he went to the stake and a late but finally glorious martyrdom.

Prayer to Christ is natural at some times to most believers, as well as to children and simple people, for He is man and has experienced immediately and in full reality human sufferings, disappointments, injustices, misunderstandings, and—it may be—uncertainty, as well as "the sharpness of death."[1] There can be no objection to such prayer, provided its proper background in the doctrine of the Trinity is clear and is kept in mind. The Tenth Anathema of the by no means wholly praiseworthy Fifth General Council of A.D. 553 is apropos and helpful in this connection:

> If anyone does not confess that our Lord Jesus Christ who was crucified in the flesh is true God and the Lord of Glory and one of the Holy Trinity: let him be anathema.

Prayer to the Holy Spirit has never come very naturally to Christian believers and is used infrequently. There is such a prayer in the American *Office of Institution of Ministers*

[1] *Te Deum.*

into Parishes or Churches, which the English Prayer Book is the poorer for not having. Its origin I have never been able to trace.[1] It reads:

> O God, Holy Ghost, Sanctifier of the faithful, visit, we pray thee, this Congregation with thy love and favour; enlighten their minds more and more with the light of the everlasting Gospel; graft in their hearts a love of the truth; increase in them true religion; nourish them with all goodness; and of thy great mercy keep them in the same, O blessed Spirit, whom, with the Father and the Son together, we worship and glorify as one God, world without end.

Also the direct invocation of the Holy Spirit at the time of the laying on of hands in ordination is well established and has ancient precedent behind it. I believe that we ought to go further and in our practice of private meditation, Bible reading, and prayer learn to invoke regularly and confidently God the Holy Spirit. It is true that He is spoken of in the New Testament as sent by the Son and as speaking not of Himself, but this is true equally of the Son in relation to the Father. Yet both are distinct, subsistent Divine Persons, partaking fully of the one Divine mind and moved perfectly by the one Divine will. And it is God the Holy Spirit who in His distinct operation and presence is closest to us and most completely within us. "Know ye not," asks St. Paul of the Corinthian Christians, "that ye are a temple of God, and that the Spirit of God dwelleth in you?"[2] It would seem to follow that personal prayer directed to the Spirit (not with any thought of "dividing the substance" or one being of God) has a special propriety and place in the economy of Christian devotion. And, if so, we cannot doubt that such prayer is pleasing to God the Holy and Undivided Trinity in whom all things are possessed in common with the actuality of a perfect communion.

4. CHRISTIAN FREEDOM

We live in a time when there is much talk of freedom. Nor would any right-thinking person speak slightingly of freedom, however negative and without content the idea of it entertained by the many is. The world has had too narrow an escape from a scientifically implemented Pharao-

---

[1] *Cf.* Collect, Seventh Sunday after Trinity.
[2] 1 Corinthians iii. 17, vi. 19 shows that the same metaphor can be applied by the Apostle to the individual human body.

ism (Cæsarism is too benign a term; so we coin one) to make it allowable for even generally correct critics of democratic institutions to disparage the fundamental human rights and liberties. Yet we live in a time when human bondage is a widespread and terrifying condition. All about us are people who should be free, but who in fact are bound. They are the prey of anxious fears, disordered desires, inordinate passions or lusts (which are of the soul and the mind as much or more than of the body), unconquerable apathies, and untrammelled and unexamined self-centredness.

How many people do you know who are really happy? How many who have discovered in living the deep power of joy? How many who have attained an interior peace that in St. Paul's great metaphor of Philippians iv. 7 stands guard like a sentry over their feelings and thoughts as the storms and tumults of life beat against and seek to invade the recesses of their souls? Yet these qualities—happiness, joy, peace, spiritual liberty—should be in some real degree the possession of every Christian.

They were the marks of the early Christians. The New Testament throughout is an eloquent testimony to the acquisition by ordinary, weak, restless, weary, disillusioned folk of great liberating spiritual qualities. To take one illustration, the New Testament is a collection of writings that deal with one theme and one only, the Christian religion. Religion is supposed to be concerned with what the Book of Common Prayer, following the Epistle to Titus, calls "a godly, righteous, and sober life." It sounds formidably serious. The poetry of Homer, on the other hand, is about Greek gods and heroes. It springs out of the youthful prime of perhaps the most gifted people yet brought into existence by Almighty God. The plays and poems of Shakespeare, likewise, are a product of a buoyant and zestful, a life-affirming age—the high Renaissance. Yet an acquaintance of mine has found out, using concordances, that the word "joy" occurs in the New Testament more than twice as often, relatively, as it does in Homer, and more than one and one half times oftener, again in terms of relative frequency, than in Shakespeare, including his comedies and love poetry. This is surely a fact worth pondering.

What was it that gave the early Christians, naturally oppressed along with their contemporaries by fear and unhappiness and a sense of unmeaning Fate, freedom and spontaneity and joy and a temper of spiritual victory? The answer admits of no doubt. The source of the transformation was, immediately, the Spirit of Divine energy and vitality—the Lord and Life-giver. But behind the activity of this Spirit, who ever proceeds from the Father and from (or through) the Son, was a free gift to the world—the gift of the only begotten Son of God, the Beloved of the eternal Father, to a lost and ruined world. And behind the coming into history of God in the Person of the uncreated Son was the love of the Father, the love of God Himself, ineffably shared by and at the same time binding together in a perfect and indivisible unity the Persons of the Blessed Trinity.

The love of God, expressing itself in relation to the world as the grace (royal favour freely given) of the Lord Jesus Christ and as the inwardly and corporately operative energy and life of the Spirit! This is the secret of the release and liberation which Christianity brought to the world. It is also the comprehensive summary of Christianity both as the action and the speech of God in history and as the sufficient clue to the vision of His eternal nature as love, knowledge and power. It is the key to realizing personally and recovering within the Church the freedom and spontaneity and abundant richness that pertain to life in Christ by the Holy Spirit.

In particular, such realization and recovery hinge upon the effectual operation of the Spirit. The doctrine of the Holy Spirit is the most powerful doctrine of the Christian religion. It is also the most neglected, partly because it is inherently intangible and mysterious, partly because its understanding hinges on a right apprehension of the Incarnation of God in Jesus Christ and of the relations of the Son alike to the Father and to the Spirit. Yet the Spirit is the key to energy, freedom, and peace in living. He is the secret weapon of the Christian in his ghostly warfare and in his temporal pilgrimage. To find Him present and to feel His Divine operation within one's life and whole being is the final aspect of Christian devotion.

When Jesus Christ sent His disciples out through all

Judea to extend His personal mission of preaching the kingdom of God and healing "all manner of disease, and all manner of sickness," He warned them of opposition and difficulty. Even though they should be "wise as serpents, and harmless as doves," they must expect to be delivered up to the councils and brought before governors and kings for His sake. "But," he assured them, "when they shall deliver you up, be not anxious how or what ye shall speak: for it shall be given you in that hour what ye shall speak. For it is not ye that speak, but the Spirit of your Father that speaketh in you."[1]

On another occasion Jesus was accused by the Scribes and Pharisees of casting out demons by the power of Beelzebub, the prince of demons. After answering the charge in a logical manner, and asserting the integrity of the offensive against evil which He as the spearhead of a new advance of the kingdom of God was leading, He turned upon his critics—the most religious men legally and outwardly of the era—and said:

> Every sin and blasphemy shall be forgiven unto men: but the blasphemy against the Spirit shall not be forgiven. And whosoever speaketh a word against the Son of man, it shall be forgiven him: but whosoever speaketh against the Holy Spirit, it shall not be forgiven him, neither in this world nor in the one to come.[2]

These words have been the occasion of much controversy and confusion in Christian history. Yet they are on the face of it a weighty and momentous utterance, and they are not without a substantial and lucid context in the total teaching of Holy Scripture with respect to the Spirit of God.[3] They underline the fact that it is in a special way the Holy Spirit with whom we are in direct and immediate contact, and that He is the author in us of all that is holy and humble and pure and sincere. It is by His operation that there actually do proceed in us from God holy desires, good counsels, and just works.[4] Were we to turn against the Spirit, refuse all His Divine promptings, and say in effect, "Be gone; I will live by a different spirit; Evil, be thou

[1] Matthew xi. 1-20.   [2] Matthew xii. 22-32.
[3] Cf., in addition to the exposition of the Spirit above in Chapter III, Isaiah lxiii. 8-11.
[4] Collect for Peace in The Order of Daily Evening Prayer (Prayer Book).

my good," we should have sold our birthright of spiritual liberty and forfeited our souls.

Men have always known that such a disaster could overtake the human spirit. This is the meaning of the Faust legend. But modern man, in his enchantment with positive reality (positivism) and his excitement and newly aroused carnal pride over evolution, became very somnolent with respect to such a possibility. It was perhaps only a legend, the reminiscence of a bad racial dream. From this lethargy bordering on sleep modern man has been rudely awakened. He knows now certainly that the Holy Spirit can leave a soul and that a Satanic spirit can enter in and take possession in His place. We have seen it happen. The newspapers of 1945 are here at one in their testimony with the Holy Bible.

The blasphemy against the Holy Spirit, then, means at least this: that integrity and sincerity of inward being are the foundation of everything wholesome and fruitful and satisfying, and that the only unforgivable sin is the admission of a spirit of fundamental irreligiousness and rejection of responsibility to God and man. Furthermore, lest we think only of the more spectacular wickedness of our time and of peculiarly formidable and terrifying instances of the forfeiture, seemingly, of the very image of humanity, we shall do well to remember that Jesus Christ had in mind the leaven of hypocrisy of the Scribes and Pharisees. This hypocrisy was in part, it seems certain, an unconscious and subtle corruption and was not incompatible with a serious and burdensome observance of religion. These words, therefore, are addressed to religious and Christian souls as much as to the indifferent and unthinking multitudes in our world and open and notorious sinners. "Wherefore let him that thinketh he standeth take heed lest he fall."[1]

---

[1] 1 Corinthians x. 12.

And that, by the way, is perhaps the most important difference between Christianity and all other religions—that in Christianity God is not a static *thing*—not even a person—but a dynamic, pulsating activity, a life, almost a kind of drama. Almost, if you won't think me irreverent, a kind of dance. . . . The whole dance or drama, or pattern of this three-Personal life is to be played out in each one of us: or (putting it the other way round) each one of us has got to enter that pattern, take his place in that dance.

C. S. Lewis: *Beyond Personality.*

And the glory which thou hast given to me I have given to them. We know now what that glory is—absolute love in perfect self-expression; this, in face of the selfishness of the world, is the Cross. . . . The purpose and consequence of that gift of *glory* is that the unity of the Godhead may be reproduced in them—in us—*that they may be one as we are one.* . . . That fellowship of love is the end for which we were created and for which our nature as God fashioned it is designed.

William Temple: *Readings in St. John's Gospel.*

It is not as a Philosopher but as Prometheus, that we worship Christ—the Man who came down from Heaven to give men the Divine Fire.

F. C. Burkitt: *Jesus Christ.*

Jesus said: "Wouldst thou love one who never died
For thee, or ever die for one who had not died for thee?
And if God dieth not for Man and giveth not himself
Eternally for Man, Man could not exist; for Man is Love
As God is Love; every kindness to another is a little Death
In the Divine Image, nor can Man exist but by Brotherhood."

William Blake: *Jerusalem.*

Nothing great in the world has been accomplished without passion.

Hegel.

CHAPTER VI

Worship, Action and the Trinity

LIFE, as we human beings ordinarily live it, is divided into play and work. That is to say, our waking life is. Roughly, one-third of it is spent in sleep. The order of words "play and work" is deliberate. In infancy play predominates. Work is pretty well confined to the effort of eating, and later to such small tasks as may be assigned to us. With the period of schooling work comes more and more into the picture. Progressively the ratio of play to work is altered and in the normal adult life is inverted. If, however, this inversion goes too far, the balance of nature is upset and there is danger of a certain warping of life. Play is an essential element of the good life. The danger of the specialist is that he will lose the ability to play. Probably this is not the danger of the masses of the people. Amusements remain the greatest business of all time. Liquor and tobacco run a close second. The problem of the ordinary person is making his work *creative* and his leisure or play genuinely *re-creative*.

Both may be, and should be, approached religiously. Religion is not simply a small segment of life, but is a dimension that should intersect and affect all life. God, we are taught in the Holy Bible, is a worker. The ancient Jews thought of the Creator as having rested on the seventh day after the labour and ardour of His infinite creative effort.[1] In the Gospel according to St. John the Christ says, in reply to criticism of Him for making a man whole on the Sabbath: "My Father worketh even until now, and I work."[2] Whether there is anything in the experience of God, who is both perfect energy and perfect rest, that corresponds to what we human beings know as work and rest, who shall say? Perhaps the idea as applied to God is pure mythology. Yet it seems to convey more and to be more nearly true than to say nothing. In any case, it is certain that we are created not for idleness, but for activity; not for sloth and the laying waste of our powers in stagnation, but for the exertion in creative ways of our best and finest energies.

[1] Genesis ii. 2-3.   [2] v. 17.

9

The same points apply to play or recreation. Whether there is validity in the conception of a kind of Divine play, or, as Mr. C. S. Lewis has put it, a "drama" or a "dance" that is the Trinitarian life of God (see quotation at the head of this chapter), is not an easy question to answer meaningfully. But of us men and women there is no question. It is one of the marks of our humanity, which is at once, and in the most paradoxical and astonishing combination, godlike and creaturely, that we need to play. We must find diversion or relaxation, and mix them with labour, if we are to keep healthy in body and wholesome or whole in mind and spirit. To accept and act upon this human necessity is, or may be, one mark of genuine humility.

This is the thesis of a great artist and thinker, Sören Kierkegaard, in his famous parable of the religious man and the Deer Park (or Zoo). Kierkegaard was an intensely religious and a deeply serious individual. It is doubtful whether anyone in the nineteenth century took himself more seriously. Indeed, some would say that he carried his idea of a special vocation of Christian suffering and witness to a point of extreme absurdity—if, indeed, he was not a pathological case. He wrestled as hardly anyone had for centuries—like Jacob of old at the ford of Jabbok—with a God who was not an idea, not a blind impersonal force, not the structure of the particular universe that is, but a tremendous personal reality, a living Lord who calls on men to decide with courage and faith for Him. In a phrase that has made theological history in the twentieth century, although it was actually called forth by Hegelian idealism a hundred years ago, Kierkegaard declared that between God and man there is an infinite qualitative distinction. It is in speaking to this favourite point that he expounds and illustrates humility or "the form of the absolute difference" between God and man. If humility is accepted, it carries with it diversion as an element in life.

There are thus two ways disclosed to deliberation: the way of humble diversion and the way of desperate exertion, the way to the Deer Park and the way to the cloister. To the Deer Park? Oh, yes, let me mention only this, though I might just as well name much else that comes under the same classification. A fool will doubtless laugh at this thought, and a priggish individual will feel offended, and both will serve as proof that the thought has validity. . . .

Our religious individual chooses the way to the Deer Park, and why? Because he does not dare to choose the way to the cloister. And why does he not dare? Because it is too high-flown. So then he takes the outing. "But does he enjoy himself?" someone will say. Oh, yes, he certainly does. And why does he enjoy himself? Because it is the humblest expression for his God-relationship to admit his humanity, and because it is human to enjoy oneself.

There is much wisdom in this superbly ironic passage. Only it is as religious persons, not as frivolous abdicators of moral and mental responsibility, that we should value and use the opportunities for amusement and play that God the creator has provided in His varied, rich and absorbing world.

Turning now to religion as a specific aspect of life and experience, in contrast to life as a whole, we may say that it likewise has two moments. It is divided into two parts. These parts are worship and action.

1. WORSHIP AND THE TRINITY

Worship is to religion what play or recreation is to ordinary living. It is the moment of pause, or rest, of renewal, of the recharging of the currents and energies of the soul. It is recreation in its supreme form.

But how does worship differ from other forms of recreation? A partial answer is that it is directed toward a responsive and personal object. It has as its object One who is also a subject. But this is true also of other forms of experience with a recreational aspect: for example, friendship and love.

These experiences at their highest have in them a recreative power. They involve rest as well as motion, peace as well as passion, the beauty of harmony as well as the disorder of inward turbulence. And they have in each case an object that is also a subject. Their very essence as a form of experience is reciprocity, mutuality, communion. It is for this reason that they offer the closest analogy which we have to worship, although such analogy is only approximate and is also far from comprehensive.

Worship is the direction of the whole self toward an infinite object—a Being that is infinite in worth, in beauty, in greatness, in power, and in glory. This Divine object is also a subject—a Spirit, a Mind, an "I." Otherwise God would not be infinite in any meaningful sense, and He would not be truly worshipful. The last word on this issue from a logical and philosophical standpoint was said long ago by Plato:

> And, O heavens, can we ever be made to believe that motion and soul and mind are not present with absolute Being? Can we imagine Being to be devoid of life and mind, and to remain in awful unmeaningness, an everlasting fixture?

When we turn to the Bible, part of its impressiveness is the serene assumption that the God of the universe is a living Lord, a "Thou" with whom the spirit of man can have a mutually meaningful encounter, as well as an "Other" who in his holiness and majesty transcends inconceivably all that we can imagine or think.

> But now thus saith the Lord that created thee, O Jacob, and he that formed thee, O Israel, Fear not: for I have redeemed thee, I have called thee by thy name: thou art mine. . . . I will say to the North, Give up; and to the South, Keep not back: bring my sons from afar, and my daughters from the end of the earth; even every one that is called by my name: for I have created him for my glory, I have formed him; yea, I have made him.[1]
>
> But will God in very deed dwell with men on the earth? Behold, heaven and the heaven of heavens cannot contain thee; how much less this house that I have built. . . . If they sin against thee (for there is no man which sinneth not), and thou be angry with them, and deliver them over before their enemies, and they carry them away captives unto a land far off or near; yet if they bethink themselves in the land whither they are carried captive, and turn and pray unto thee in the land of their captivity, saying, We have sinned, we have done amiss, and have dealt wickedly; . . . Then hear thou from the heavens, even from thy dwelling place, their prayer and supplications, and maintain their cause, and forgive thy people which have sinned against thee.[2]
>
> When ye pray, use not vain repetitions, as the heathen do: for they think that they shall be heard for their much speaking. Be ye not like unto them: for your Father knoweth what things ye have need of, before ye ask him.[3]

True religion is relationship. It is being related in a living way to the living God. This is the assumption behind and implicit in all Biblical and Christian thought, worship and life. But our relation to God has in it dimensions that no other relation has. It has in it altitudes and depths and ranges and horizons that are without any precise parallel in human

[1] Isaiah xliii. 1, 6-7. [2] 2 Chronicles vi. 18, 36-37, 39.
[3] Matthew vi. 7-8.

things. One of these dimensions is adoration or the giving expression in feeling, thought, and words to our sense of the immeasurable greatness, goodness and beauty of God.

Worship is adoration. It is love and homage and reverence. It is also praise and thanksgiving. It is confession. It is communion, in silence and in speech. It is fellowship with the Infinite Mystery, with the Inconceivable Ultimate, whom men name "God," and whom Christians call "Father" because Jesus Christ has so taught them and because—far more—this God has come out in Christ to meet them and to take them by the hand and to conduct them lovingly to their Father's house.

Worship, then, is adoration and communion. As such it includes words in many forms. But it is more. It takes up in it the whole created world in its splendour and wonder, and the world of human art at its highest as well. Two of the Proper Psalms for Trinity Sunday bring this out in a striking manner:

> The voice of the Lord is upon the waters: the glory of God thundereth: the Lord is upon many waters.[1]
> Praise him with the sound of the trumpet: praise him with the psaltery and harp. Praise him with the timbrel and dance: praise him with stringed instruments and organs. Praise him upon the loud cymbals: praise him upon the high sounding cymbals.[2]

The whole creation is in a sense a hymn or an anthem of praise. There is glory in all being, enhanced by the very varieties and graduations and contrasting perfections that go to make up the totality of created existence. This is relevant to Christian worship. It is the God of the universe whom we adore—the mighty being without whom nothing would exist, apart from whose fiat there would be only vacancy and nothingness. We need to keep before our minds the greatness and the attractiveness and the fascination and mystery and infinitude of God. We ought not to associate God simply with the Church or Sunday or saying prayers; we should not feel He is a monopoly of ecclesiastics. Parochialism is a danger in theology as well as in Church life. This is not the spirit of the New Testament. Even in the Book of Revelation, where the author seeks to lift the vision of his readers away from this world in all its

---

[1] xxix. 3.   [2] cl. 4-5.

evil and agony and suffering up to the heavenly city, the realm of everlasting peace, there is the sense of God the Creator.

> The four and twenty elders fall down before him that sat on the throne, and worship him that liveth for ever and ever, and cast their crowns before the throne, saying, Thou art worthy, O Lord, to receive glory and honour and power: for thou hast created all things, and for thy pleasure they are, and were created.[1]

The *Te Deum* sounds at the outset a similar note:

> We praise thee, O God; we acknowledge thee to be the Lord.
> All the earth doth worship thee: the Father everlasting.

Reginald Heber in his inspired hymn makes explicit the connection between the element of the creatorship of God in worship and the ascription of all praise to the Blessed Trinity.

> Holy, Holy, Holy! Lord God Almighty!
> All thy works shall praise thy Name,
>   In earth, and sky, and sea;
> Holy, Holy, Holy! merciful and mighty!
> God in Three Persons, blessed Trinity.

It was, however, not from the creation, or even from the Old Testament, that Heber derived this association of the two things: the creation and the Trinity. It was from the fact that he was thinking of God as He has made Himself known in the Christian revelation. This revelation includes the Old Testament with its dominating idea of the activity of God in nature and history. But it adds to the Divine majesty the Divine humility and condescension in Jesus Christ. It adds the love poured out sacrificially and costingly in the Son upon His lonely Cross and communicated lavishly and bindingly and powerfully in the outpouring of the Holy Spirit upon the assembly ("church" means literally "assembly") of Christians at Pentecost. This Spirit later Christians were to call the love of the Father and the Son. It was a love that when it came upon them seemed to the Christians to be like tongues of flame, so ardently did it inflame them, so close did it knit and bind them in one communion and fellowship, as in a mystical Divine body.

---

[1] iv. 10-11. (These verses are the conclusion of the Epistle for Trinity Sunday.)

Christian worship is directed to the Christian God. It is the adoration of God as He is apprehended and experienced by the Church—the company, society, assembly, and fellowship of the faithful. This apprehension has always taken a trinal form. The Baptismal Formula in St. Matthew's Gospel is evidence of this. And it but summarizes formally the scattered and unsystematized thought and language of the whole New Testament. The same is true for us. We know that God remains the Creator, the Redeemer, and the Sanctifier or Strengthener—the Comforter. And if this sums up adequately what God has done and continues to do, it must also tell us something about His being—about what He is in Himself. For the thing that is ultimate in a person—the thing that you and I want to know about even in human things—is nature and character. We want to know what a person is. If we know this, we can judge without difficulty his actions. So Christians believe that God not only seems to be, but actually is, a Trinitarian God, and they say continually as they offer in company with their fellows praise and adoration to the God of the universe:

Glory be to the Father, and to the Son, and to the Holy Ghost; as it was in the beginning, is now, and ever shall be, world without end.

There is one further and last point. The Christian religion teaches us that "God is Love." This is the boldest and most radical statement in the history of philosophy and theology. It is a tremendous assertion. "God is Love."

What does it mean? It means, of course, that God has acted lovingly. He has intervened and is for ever intervening to redeem mankind from sin, error, blindness and folly. He has acted and is for ever acting to sustain and strengthen and enlighten faithful men. But why? Because He is in Himself, apart from and without any necessary connection with the creation, Love—pure, disinterested, ardent, selfless Love. He is a social being. He is within the unity of a single, perfect, individual life a Trinity of persons—the Father, the Son, and the Holy Spirit.

This is the God whom we worship—a God who is in Himself Love, though in a manner, of course, inconceivably greater and higher than we can imagine. Such a God—a personal God, a God who loves because He is Love—

alone can call out the highest response in us His creatures. For there is none other so worshipful, so truly adorable, so everlastingly praiseworthy, so rightly to be magnified, so properly the One to whom we lift up our hearts.

God in three persons, Blessed Trinity.
To Him be all glory, praise, might, majesty, dominion, and love, for ever and ever!

2. ACTION AND THE HOLY TRINITY

If you happen to be a lover and appreciator of great music, and are accustomed to attend many symphony concerts, it is very likely that you will come away from a concert full of the beauty and emotional stimulus of the music. You will possibly exclaim, "That is really great!" You might even quote the lines of one of the premier devotees of beauty so far produced by the human race:

> Beauty is truth, truth beauty—that is all
> Ye know on earth, and all ye need to know.

Or those lines written earlier on the same theme:

> A thing of beauty is a joy for ever:
> Its loveliness increases; it will never
> Pass into nothingness; but still will keep
> A bower quiet for us, and a sleep
> Full of sweet dreams, and health, and quiet breathing,
> . . . Yes, in spite of all,
> Some shape of beauty moves away the pall
> From our dark spirits.

But you will not come away from hearing a symphony with a stronger sense of duty and a felt impulse to action. You will not come away with the consciousness of a will renewed and invigorated.

With Christian worship it is otherwise. Worship may indeed do, and should do, psychologically, what music does for many people. It may give a sense of purification and inward cleansing. It may accomplish, in Aristotle's famous phrase, applied by him to tragic drama, "a catharsis of the emotions," purging the soul from all that is sordid and mean and base. This is a part of genuine recreation. Sacramental worship, especially, commemorating and mystically re-enacting as it does the drama of our redemption, is *re-creative* in the highest sense.

But worship, inclusive of hearing the Word of God read and preached, does more than purify and renew. It generates also an impulse to action. It is a conveyer of the deed. It is a conductor to decision.

This active impulse may be of different kinds. It may be an enkindling of love, good will, and respect toward one's fellow-men. It may be a dream of a better and kinder world —a world in which the kingdom or reign of God for which Christians pray continually is realized more fully. It may be a resolve to act more courageously and gallantly in relation to one's life problems, whatever they may be, whether trials or temptations or failures or sufferings or the demands and challenges and hazards of large opportunities thrust upon us.

Why this difference between the æsthetic approach to life, as symbolized in our illustration of the symphony, and the religious approach? Because religion is concerned with life as a whole, and life is in large part, of very necessity, action. Even if we do not act, we do act. If we postpone or evade decision, we thereby decide. And destiny is not seldom involved in those colourless negative acts and decisions.

But even more there is a difference between the æsthetic and the religious approaches to life because God is Himself living and active, because He is creative will. It is the kind of God we worship that in the end determines our character, shapes our ends, and directs our active life. We become like that which we really love and adore and desire and honour and serve.

Now it is in His activity that the Lord of this universe, the one, only, and true God, has made Himself known in a threefold manner—as Father, as Son, and as the Holy Spirit—as a Trinity. "In the beginning God created the heavens and the earth." God sent into the world His only begotten Son, not to condemn the world, but that the world—God's world—might be saved through Him. After the Son, through His death and passion, resurrection and ascension, had made complete our redemption, another Comforter or Strengthener, the Spirit of the Lord, the Holy Ghost, was sent to endow and energize the Church and to be the sanctifier or builder-up in holiness of the faithful.

This is the action of God. This is what God has done and is doing for His world and for us. As with human beings, the reasons for His acts are rooted in His being or nature; and this is far more perfectly true of God than it is even of the most mature and fully formed and seemingly integrated human personality, since God is eternal and unchanging, whereas man is finite and for ever subject to the strains and pressures and shocks and storms of this mortal life. God's acts in creation, redemption, and sanctification are expressions of a loving purpose; they show us a God whose activity is one of self-giving, self-emptying, self-communication, self-sacrifice. It was the discovery of this that made Christianity a new religion with a distinctive and powerful Gospel—the Gospel of Divine Love. But such a Gospel has validity, once we have begun to think about it and analyze it rationally, only as Divine action in time is seen to be the expression of a Divine Love that is eternal, that is of the very nature of absolute and unchanging Deity. Hence St. John's assertion that "God is Love" is the ultimate simple summary of the Christian Gospel, which is first of all a résumé and an announcement of the acts of God. This assertion, furthermore, involves the doctrine that God is in Himself a Trinity of persons; otherwise we make God dependent upon the created world and we have no explanation for the fact that He has acted and spoken, or revealed Himself, in a threefold way and with, we might say, a threefold Divine signature. Or, if this sounds technical, God has made Himself known in Christ as more than Jehovah—the ancient sacred name revealed to Moses and believed to mean "I-am-that-I-am." He has made Himself known as Father, Son, and Holy Ghost; and it is in this new and—Christians believe—final threefold name that we are baptized and born anew into the family and people of God—the Church.

Thus we can see that the doctrine of the Trinity, though it may seem a complicated and difficult doctrine, is both the key to Christian worship and the foundation of Christian action.

In conclusion, with the utmost definiteness and realism in facing and grappling with the actual world and the existence of men and women in the twentieth century, let us examine the applicableness and practicality of this general exposition of action and the Holy Trinity.

The greatest need in the world is not economic or political or technical. It is not better planning. It is not even bread, although Christianity among all the world's religions and "spiritual" philosophies makes the most of the body and hence of food and medicine and housing and economics in general. It is faith, and the vision and strength and peace and release from self-centredness that faith in the Christian God—a God of love—alone can give. This need can only be met by preaching the Gospel "in demonstration of the Spirit and of power"[1] at home and everywhere throughout the world. To meet this need is the primary mission of the Church. It is the first call to Christian action.

Now the word "missions" rubs many people, even many very sincere religious people, the wrong way. But missions comes from "mission," and "mission" means being sent. The idea of sending is of the very fabric of Christianity. The Father sends the Son. The Son after His death and passion and resurrection breathes upon His disciples the Holy Spirit—the Divine Breath—and says to them: "As My Father hath sent Me, so send I you."[2] Yes, Christianity begins with the heavenly conceived and heavenly initiated mission of the eternal Son of God, and it ends with our being sent into Christian vocations even as ordinary lay folk and with our helping to send others—missionaries we call them—to the ends of the earth. Christianity is missions. The faith of the Divine Trinity means, if it means anything, energy and ardour in sending Christian evangelists and prophets and physicians. Such sending is the imitation of God.

Then Christianity means action in the community, the nation, the world. It means social action. Now whether we like it or not, we are all citizens. "Man," said Aristotle, "is a political animal." We are born into society, and we cannot escape society and social obligations. German intellectuals like Thomas Mann, according to his own confession, tried to live as purely private persons, paying no heed to politics. Karl Barth, in his early preaching and teaching, led a revival of the orthodox Christian conceptions in their rele-

---

[1] 1 Corinthians ii. 4.   [2] John xx. 21.

vance to the universal problems of human existence. This revival stirred, first, the German-speaking Churches of Europe, particularly in Germany, in the decade following the First World War, and then the Churches of Britain and America. Much power was generated by this movement, and it may be that Barth's influence was a principal factor in the pre-eminence of the Christian Church throughout Europe as a centre of resistance to German totalitarianism. For this witness, in a day of judgment, of Churches and of Churchmen, both Protestant and Catholic, no Christian can be too grateful. But Barth, by calling men's attention, at first, too exclusively to heaven, eternity, and the mysterious otherness of God, caused German Christians to join with literati and intellectuals generally in leaving politics to the Devil and Adolph Hitler.

This is a warning to all Christians. Society is with us. Politics may be disagreeable, but they are ever with us. The only question is, "What kind of society do we want?" "What kind of government do we want?" "What kind of education do we want?" Or, to put the matter another way, "What is the aim of men in society and hence of social action?"

The answer depends on our conception of God, the Ultimate Real. If God is an aloof Deity, we may aim at a rough justice animated by an enlightened self-interest. We may even talk, as so many in our democratic society are talking today continually, about the dignity of the individual. But actually this will only be a rationalization of self-concern. We shall not really care about men as our brothers. How can we, if the will to brotherhood among men is only a human idea? If God be an infinite tyrant, cold, implacable, and arbitrary, then we shall accept tyranny and arbitrariness as social inevitabilities. We shall look upon life as a race, a competition, a struggle. Might is right. Let the weak go to the wall. The world belongs to the master race, the class is power, the truly forceful and dominating leader. In National Socialist Germany we see the working out, with a pitilessness which only logic coupled with possession by Satan himself could generate, of this idea of God or the Supreme Real. It does not matter whether such a Being was addressed in public invocation, as by Hitler, or identified with nature and Darwinian evolution, as by Rosenberg and his pupils, two of whom told me in August, 1939, ten days before the invasion of Poland, that they were not atheists like the Communists, but that they did not believe God to be personal and they did not believe in sin. They added that the laws of nature were the commandments of God: no others have been or can be given to men.

But if Christianity is true—if Jesus Christ was very God of very God made man—and if His pure love and will to sacrifice was an expression in temporal act of the eternal social life of God, then love must inform justice, brotherhood is a fundamental political principle, and the goal of all society, in the family, the city, the nation-state, the world, is fellowship and co-operation. Yes, we may even say, we are bound to say, the issue of the Trinitarian being of God is crucial for the Charter and League or Association of the United Nations now in painful process of being brought to birth. It is paramount in decisiveness for all international as well as intranational and interpersonal relations and questions. For when we confess the faith of the Church in the Holy Trinity, we affirm our belief that God is Himself the archetype of all community, all fellowship, all love.

If this belief is true, if ultimate being and supreme reality is the Trinity in Unity, then we shall never rest content with a new paper League of Nations. We shall not put our trust in formulas and blueprints, or even in promises set down solemnly and impressively in ink, but extracted out of expediency and a shifting opportunism. We shall put our faith in the power of Divine love, and we shall seek to bring the Spirit of love and the Source of fellowship into a fruitful connection and commerce with the idea of justice. Men are at the present moment in the way of recovering some sense of this great idea that has made history since the days of Plato, and Socrates and Æschylus before him. Justice is, and will remain, the cardinal, immediately relevant political virtue.

But if Christianity is true, we cannot stop with justice even in relation to our enemies. Christ's commandment is that we should love them and desire to forgive them and see them restored to integrity and self-respect and the pre-

cious sense of being fellow-possessors of a common humanity. Still more is it impossible to come to rest in relation to
our allies and international comrades with correctness and
the letter of upright dealings. Love is the ultimate Christian
virtue and idea, and it must inform and transform other
virtues and ideas and traditions and social procedures.
Furthermore is it as clear as the noonday sun that justice
without love cannot stand uncorrupted in the state or in
international relations or in the lesser and more inward
circles of human relatedness. It is not self-sufficing as a
human and ideal sentiment. It is unable of itself to offer
effectual resistance to the seductions of place and power as
they surround the seats of the mighty or to the solicitations
of desire for special privilege as they well up spontaneously
in the hearts of the citizenry of a democracy.

From this standpoint the Christian doctrine of Love is as
far removed as possible from the cloudlands of the chimer-
ical and the impractical. It is as real and as pertinent to the
life of the world in this day of its hot and dusty march as the
cool waters of a well in an oasis are to soldiers who are compelled to push on relentlessly across a dry and arid desert.
"All our doings without charity are nothing worth." This
is not only true on the Sunday next before Lent once every
year. It is not only the ultimate teaching of the Christian
religion, grounded in the very nature of God Himself. It
is a final principle and standard of all human life, which if
men will deny and set at naught they shall find that they
have embraced death.

Last of all there is the question, underlying all others, of
our will not only to believe but to act. There is the question,
crucial for everything written in this little book, of the
psychological springs of human action. On this, in one way
or another, a good deal has been said. Yet, looking back, I
am aware that I have only hacked away here and there at
the sculpture of a vast and majestic theme. If, however,
this slight essay on the gorgeous subject of the Trinity and
Christian Devotion should lead someone with keener powers
and a finer chisel to perfect the work which we must now
leave, or if it should be that some are moved by this book
to rise out of lethargy and distraction to a new sense of the
miracle of Divine love and a feeling of its powerful motion

within their wills, the travail of this authorship will not
have been in vain.

As we come, writer and reader, to the end of our
meditation and thinking together, let me say simply that
there is one antidote, and one only, to the spirit of indecision in us all, to the Hamlet in every man who is wont
to soliloquize:

> To be, or not to be,—that is the question:—
>   .   .   .   .
> For who would bear the whips and scorns of time,
> The oppressor's wrong, the proud man's contumely,
> The pangs of despis'd love, the law's delay,
> The insolence of office, and the spurns
> That patient merit of the unworthy takes,
> When he himself might his quietus make
> With a bare bodkin? . . .
> But that the dread of something after death,—
> The undiscover'd country, from whose bourn
> No traveller returns,—puzzles the will,
> And makes us rather bear those ills we have
> Than fly to others that we know not of?
> Thus conscience does make cowards of us all;
> And thus the native hue of resolution
> Is sicklied o'er with the pale cast of thought:
> And enterprises of great pith and moment,
> With this regard, their currents turn awry
> And lose the name of action.

That antidote—to indecision and to the spirit of doubt,
denial and despair—is the act of the eternal Son of God
taking upon Him our flesh and finding glory not in dom-
ination or spectacular achievement, but in deliberate sacrifice unto death for you and me and every human being.
The power to carry through and endure to the end, not
wistfully and with an unredeemed and pagan nostalgia,
but joyfully and in a victorious spirit, is not our own to
achieve and to contribute, but is God the Holy Ghost, the
Spirit of the Father and the Son, within us. In His Divine
comfort (or, in old English, strength) no person need
falter or fail.

Thus through the action of the Trinitarian God, in which
action we are given an intimation also of the character of
the Divine life, we know that our mission and destiny as

human beings is not only thought and contemplation, but action and passion. In this knowledge and in the steadfast will of love that corresponds to it we become partakers also of the life of the eternal and ever-blessed God, the Father, the Son, and the Holy Spirit.